COOKBOOK

· SWEET TREATS FOR THE GEEK IN ALL OF US ·

ROSANNA PANSINO

ATRIA BOOKS

New York London Toronto Sydney New Delhi

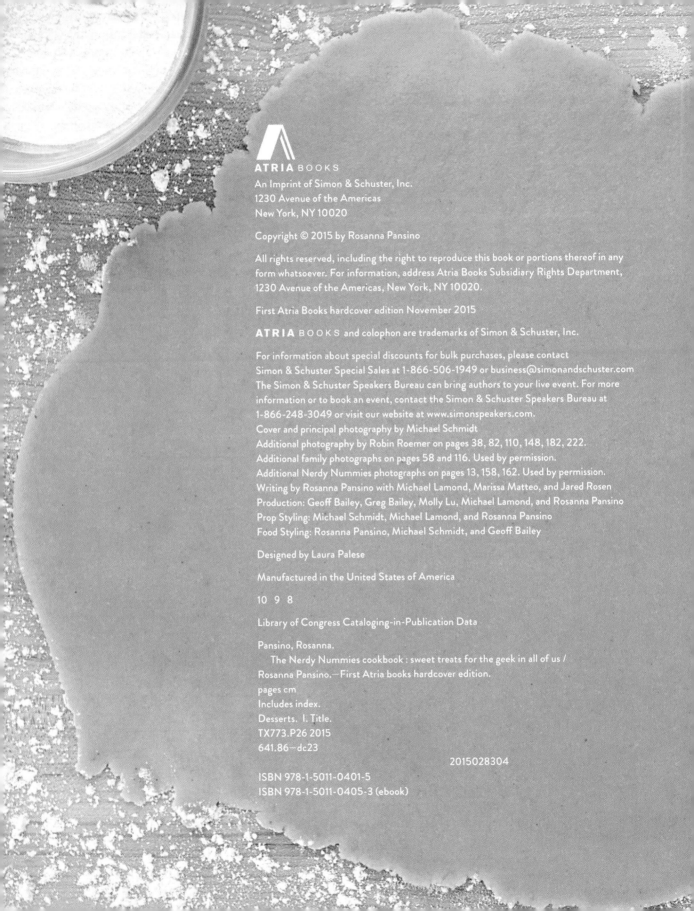

ATRIA BOOKS

An Imprint of Simon & Schuster, Inc.
1230 Avenue of the Americas
New York, NY 10020

First Atria Books hardcover edition November 2015

ATRIA BOOKS and colophon are trademarks of Simon & Schuster, Inc.

For information about special discounts for bulk purchases, please contact
Simon & Schuster Special Sales at 1-866-506-1949 or business@simonandschuster.com
The Simon & Schuster Speakers Bureau can bring authors to your live event. For more
information or to book an event, contact the Simon & Schuster Speakers Bureau at
1-866-248-3049 or visit our website at www.simonspeakers.com.

Cover and principal photography by Michael Schmidt
Additional photography by Robin Roemer on pages 38, 82, 110, 148, 182, 222.
Additional family photographs on pages 58 and 116. Used by permission.
Additional Nerdy Nummies photographs on pages 13, 158, 162. Used by permission.
Writing by Rosanna Pansino with Michael Lamond, Marissa Matteo, and Jared Rosen
Production: Geoff Bailey, Greg Bailey, Molly Lu, Michael Lamond, and Rosanna Pansino
Prop Styling: Michael Schmidt, Michael Lamond, and Rosanna Pansino
Food Styling: Rosanna Pansino, Michael Schmidt, and Geoff Bailey

Designed by Laura Palese

Manufactured in the United States of America

10 9 8

Library of Congress Cataloging-in-Publication Data

Pansino, Rosanna.
    The Nerdy Nummies cookbook : sweet treats for the geek in all of us /
Rosanna Pansino.—First Atria books hardcover edition.
    pages cm
    Includes index.
    Desserts. I. Title.
    TX773.P26 2015
    641.86—dc23
                                                    2015028304

ISBN 978-1-5011-0401-5
ISBN 978-1-5011-0405-3 (ebook)

THIS BOOK IS DEDICATED TO

ALL MY AWESOME VIEWERS

BAKERS GONNA BAKE!

· AUTHOR'S NOTE ·

I wanted to give a special thanks to Marissa Matteo for helping me through the process of making my first cookbook; her guidance and advice were invaluable every step of the way. She was present during each day of shooting over the course of several months, transcribed my baking process into steps, helped with food testing, coordinated with the entire team to keep things on track, and even drove all around town to find last-minute props. In more ways than I can put into words, her advice and calming presence truly mean the world to me.

· TABLE OF ·
CONTENTS

• INTRODUCTION •

HEY GUYS, IT'S RO! Thanks for taking the time to check out my very first cookbook! For those of you who don't know me, my name is Rosanna Pansino and I'm the creator and host of *Nerdy Nummies*, the internet's most popular baking show.

Nerdy Nummies combines two things I love with all my heart: geek culture and baking. Video games, science fiction, math, and comics were just a few of the things people considered "nerdy" when I was growing up; now they inspire every recipe you'll find inside this book. From a Periodic Table of Cupcakes to Moon Phase Macarons, there are plenty of sweet treats for the geek in all of us!

My grandmother (Nana) taught me to infuse everything I bake with love, and it's thanks to her that baking has been such an integral part of my life. Making food in the kitchen is something that has always brought my family together, and I hope you enjoy these projects as much as I enjoyed making them.

I wanted this book to be a physical embodiment of the show. Included within each chapter are a few of my favorite recipes as well as many completely new projects.

ABOUT NERDY NUMMIES

The *Nerdy Nummies* debut episode was about baking a Mario Star Cake. There wasn't a geeky-themed food show on television or the internet at that time, so after a positive response from both the online community and my friends, I decided to make it a series. With that, the original nerdy baking show was born!

In the early months of the show, I filmed, edited, and uploaded each episode completely by myself. Since I'm pretty slow at editing, releasing two videos a month was simply not keeping up with the requests of my viewers. It was because of their feedback and enthusiasm that I decided to begin making videos full-time and release them more often. Now, the *Nerdy Nummies* crew has grown to a small group of friends and family.

The internet is a truly amazing place and I feel incredibly humbled by the outpouring of support I've received over the years. Having a direct connection with people all over the world is incredible and it's why I enjoy doing *Nerdy Nummies* so much!

LEFT TO RIGHT: Matt Jones, Mama Mia, Michael Schmidt, Molly Lu, Greg Bailey, Rosanna Pansino, Geoff Bailey, Papa Pizza, Mike Lamond (HuskyStarcraft).

FUN TIMES ON THE SHOW

Here are just a few of the wonderful guests who have stopped by the *Nerdy Nummies* kitchen to share their own passion for baking!

Astrophysicist and fellow baker Neil deGrasse Tyson lived long and prospered with an awesome *Star Trek* cake; friend and digital pioneer, Michelle Phan, created a batch of Super Smash Brothers cupcakes; fitness guru Cassey Ho made healthy black bean Superhero Burgers; and comedy duo Smosh enjoyed Vegan Mini Donut Holes.

The most special guest I've ever had on the show is my dad. He has always been a huge Disney fan, and making *Frozen* Olaf treats with him is one of my fondest memories.

So without further ado, I hope you enjoy *The Nerdy Nummies Cookbook*! There's lots of baking to be done, worlds to explore, dinosaur bones to excavate, computer chips to program, and most important, cakes to eat. Let's get started!

1. Ro and Papa Pizza **2.** Ro and Neil deGrasse Tyson **3.** Ro and Michelle Phan **4.** Ro and Cassey Ho (Blogilates)
5. Ro and Smosh (Ian Hecox and Anthony Padilla)

• HOW TO USE THIS BOOK •

BASIC RECIPES

Simple and easy recipes are on pages 22–37. These can be used to complete all of the projects in this book, but feel free to use your own preferred recipes—whether from scratch or a box mix! The goal is to have fun and be creative, so work with whatever you have. I encourage you to use your favorite colors, candies, and tools to make your creations unique; there is no set way to bake!

STEP-BY-STEP PHOTOS

I have always been a very visual learner, and sometimes dyslexia makes it difficult for me to follow a large number of wordy instructions. For this reason, I have added six step-by-step photos for every project in this book (or twelve steps for a few of the more intricate ones). The images are labeled with letters to match their corresponding steps and can be used as a visual guide throughout the decorating process. Just remember, your creations don't need to look exactly like the ones in the photos. As my grandma always used to say: "Mistakes are delicious!"

TEMPLATES & QR CODES

Some of the projects use cookie cutters and fun shapes. Templates to re-create these shapes have been included on pages 252–253. To make a stencil, trace the image onto a piece of paper, then cut out the shape with scissors. Once you have your shape cut out, simply place it on your rolled out cookie dough and use a small knife to cut around the edges.

Creating a template for piping designs is also easy. Trace copies of your desired shapes onto a sheet of paper and then place wax paper over the top of it on your work surface. Pipe on your royal icing, chocolate, or Candy Melts and let set until hardened. Lastly, remove gently by hand or by sliding a sharp knife underneath.

You can also print templates by downloading the free ScanLife app at www.getscanlife.com. Or you can download all templates from NerdyNummiesCookbook.com. Using the app, hold the camera of your device a few inches from the QR codes to scan and download the files directly. These can be saved and printed at any time.

DOWNLOAD
QR reader app on your mobile device

LOOK FOR
QR code symbol throughout the book

SCAN QR CODE
and download template using the QR app

PRINT
downloaded templates

· TOOLS ·

Baking sheet

Cupcake liners

Cake lifter

Tweezers

Toothpicks

Wax paper

Lollipop sticks

Polka dot stencil

Rubber spatula

Wooden spoon

Cake tester

Pastry brush

Candy thermometer

Small and large icing spatulas

Squeeze bottle

Paintbrushes

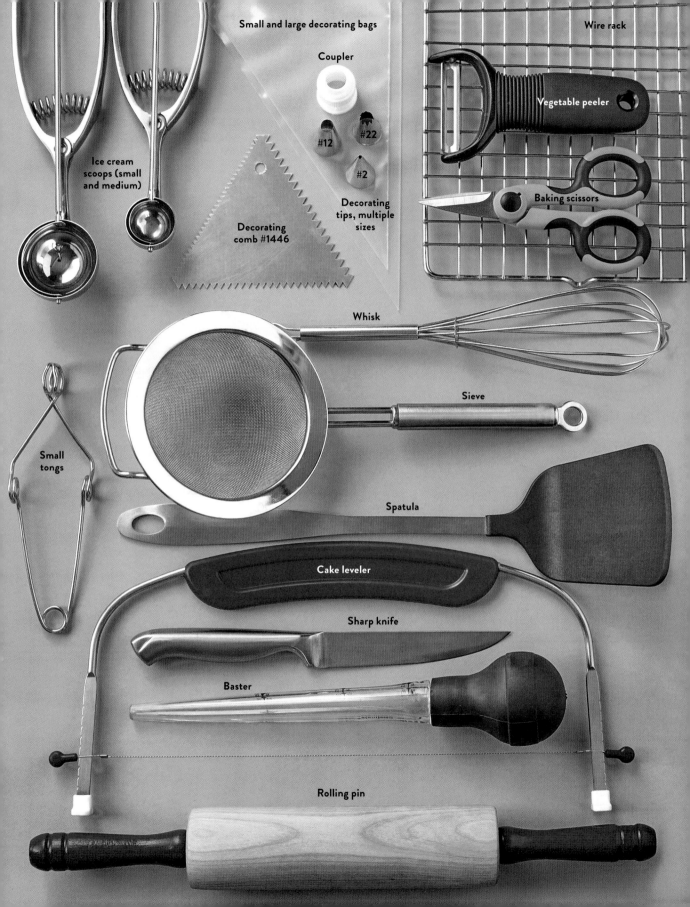

Small and large decorating bags

Coupler

#12

#22

#2

Decorating tips, multiple sizes

Decorating comb #1446

Ice cream scoops (small and medium)

Wire rack

Vegetable peeler

Baking scissors

Whisk

Sieve

Small tongs

Spatula

Cake leveler

Sharp knife

Baster

Rolling pin

• CANDY DECORATING •

M&M's Minis

Caramels

M&M's

Pastel M&M's

Reese's Pieces

Mini Lorna Doones

Chocolate coins

Sliced almonds

York Peppermint Patties Minis

Mini Oreos

Oreos

Pretzel sticks

Graham crackers

Hershey's Milk Chocolate Bar

Ghirardelli Chocolate Square

Rice Krispies Treats

Reese's Bar

Kit Kat bar

Twix

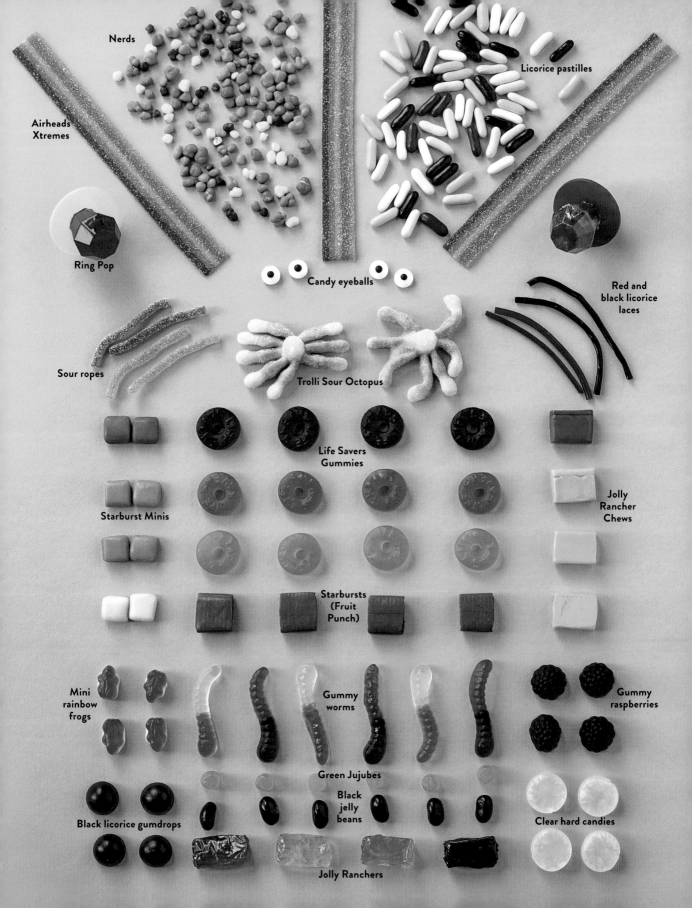

Nerds

Airheads
Xtremes

Licorice pastilles

Ring Pop

Red and
black licorice
laces

Candy eyeballs

Sour ropes

Trolli Sour Octopus

Life Savers
Gummies

Starburst Minis

Jolly
Rancher
Chews

Starbursts
(Fruit
Punch)

Mini
rainbow
frogs

Gummy
worms

Gummy
raspberries

Green Jujubes

Black licorice gumdrops

Black
jelly
beans

Clear hard candies

Jolly Ranchers

• TIPS & TECHNIQUES •

ASSEMBLING A DECORATING BAG

Insert a coupler base inside a decorating bag as far as you can.

Snip the tip of the bag even with the end of the coupler.

Place the desired decorating tip on the end of the coupler.

Screw on the coupler ring to secure the tip.

Place the decorating bag in a glass for support and fold down the edges.

Scoop in your frosting or icing until it reaches two-thirds of the way up the bag.

Unfold the edges of the bag.

Tie the bag closed (I use a small rubber band, but you can also use a twist tie) near the frosting. This prevents the frosting from coming out and also creates the best pressure and control for decorating.

COLORING FONDANT

Grease your hands with shortening (or use food-safe gloves) to prevent the food coloring from staining your hands.

Place the fondant on wax paper dusted with powdered sugar, and add drops of food coloring to the fondant.

Knead the food coloring into the fondant. If the fondant becomes too sticky as you knead it, add powdered sugar to firm it up and continue kneading.

Knead the fondant until the color is evenly blended.

DIPPING CAKE POPS

Use lollipop sticks to pre-poke holes in a foam block before dipping cake pops.

If the melted chocolate or candy is too thick (it should easily run off a spoon while leaving it thinly coated), add oil flakes or vegetable oil to thin it out.

Let excess chocolate or candy drip back into the bowl after dipping.

CHILLED CAKE POP   FROZEN CAKE POP

Temperature is important! Cake balls should be chilled, but not frozen, before dipping. If the cake ball is too cold it will crack the coating.

APPLE PIE

Makes one 9-inch pie

PIE DOUGH

2½ cups all-purpose flour
2 tablespoons granulated sugar
¼ teaspoon salt
2 sticks (8 ounces) cold salted butter, cubed
¼ to ½ cup ice water

FILLING

3½ pounds Granny Smith apples
⅓ cup granulated sugar
⅓ cup firmly packed light brown sugar
3 tablespoons all-purpose flour
1½ teaspoons ground cinnamon
¼ teaspoon ground cloves
⅛ teaspoon ground allspice
3 tablespoons lemon juice
1½ tablespoons salted butter, cubed

Egg wash: 1 egg beaten with 2 tablespoons water

1. Make the dough: Combine the flour, sugar, salt, and butter in a large bowl and mix with a hand mixer until the mixture resembles coarse meal. Add just enough ice water so the dough holds together when pinched.

2. Divide the dough in half and form two flat disks. Wrap each disk in plastic wrap and refrigerate for at least 1 hour.

3. Preheat the oven to 425°F.

4. Make the filling: Peel, core, and cut the apples into ¼-inch-thick slices. In a large bowl, whisk the sugars, flour, cinnamon, cloves, and allspice. Gently mix in the apple slices to coat. Add the lemon juice and mix again.

5. On a lightly floured surface, roll out one disk of dough to a 13-inch round about ¼ inch thick. Fit the dough into a 9-inch deep-dish pie plate. Trim the excess dough.

6. Pour the apple filling into the pie shell. Dot the cubed butter over the filling.

7. Roll out the second disk of dough about ¼ inch thick. Cut out a round the same diameter as the top of your pie plate and place on top of the pie. Crimp the edges of the dough to make a decorative trim.

8. Make slits in the top for steam to escape and brush with the egg wash. (This helps the crust turn a nice golden brown.)

9. Bake at 425°F for 15 minutes, then reduce the heat to 350°F and bake until the crust is golden brown and the juices are bubbling, about 40 minutes more.

10. Let the pie cool before serving.

BUTTER CAKE

Makes one 9 x 13-inch sheet cake or 24 cupcakes

1½ cups all-purpose flour
1 cup plus 2 tablespoons almond meal
2 teaspoons baking powder
¼ teaspoon salt
2 sticks (8 ounces) plus 2 tablespoons salted butter, at room temperature
1½ cups superfine sugar (aka baker's sugar)
2 teaspoons vanilla extract
4 large eggs
1 cup plus 2 tablespoons whole milk

1. Preheat the oven to 350°F. Grease a 9 x 13-inch metal baking pan. Line the bottom with parchment paper, grease the paper, and flour the pan. (Or see the cupcake variation below.)

2. In a large bowl, whisk together the flour, almond meal, baking powder, and salt. Set aside.

3. In a second large bowl, with an electric mixer, beat the butter until softened. Add the superfine sugar and beat until light and fluffy, 3 to 5 minutes. Scrape down the sides of the bowl as needed.

4. Beat in the vanilla.

5. Add the eggs, one at a time, beating well after each addition. Scrape down the sides of the bowl as needed.

6. On low speed, alternate adding the flour mixture and the milk to the butter mixture, beginning and ending with the flour mixture.

7. Pour the batter into the prepared pan and spread evenly. Tap the bottom of the pan on the work surface to get rid of any air bubbles.

8. Bake until a wooden pick inserted in the center comes out clean, 30 to 35 minutes.

9. Cool in the pan on a wire rack for 15 minutes. If necessary, loosen the cake from the sides of the pan with a small knife. Carefully flip the cake upside down onto the rack, peel off the parchment paper, and then turn the cake right side up onto the rack to cool completely.

Butter Cupcakes: Line 24 cups of 2 muffin tins with paper liners and fill two-thirds full with batter. (Or use 1 muffin tin and bake in two batches.) Bake at 350°F until a wooden pick inserted in the center of a cupcake comes out clean, 18 to 20 minutes. Transfer to a wire rack to cool.

POUND CAKE

Makes one 9 x 13-inch sheet cake

3½ cups all-purpose flour

1¾ teaspoons baking powder

¼ teaspoon salt

2½ sticks (10 ounces) salted butter, at room temperature

2 cups sugar

4 large eggs, at room temperature

2 tablespoons finely grated lemon zest

2 teaspoons vanilla extract

1 cup whole milk

1. Preheat the oven to 325°F. Grease a 9 x 13-inch metal baking pan. Line the bottom with parchment paper, grease the paper, and flour the pan.

2. In a medium bowl, whisk together the flour, baking powder, and salt.

3. In a large bowl, with an electric mixer, beat the butter until softened. Add the sugar and beat until light and fluffy, 3 to 5 minutes. Scrape down the sides of the bowl as needed.

4. Add the eggs, one at a time, beating well after each addition. Scrape down the sides of the bowl as needed.

5. Beat in the lemon zest and vanilla.

6. On low speed, alternate adding the flour mixture and the milk to the butter mixture, beginning and ending with the flour mixture.

7. Pour the batter into the prepared pan and spread evenly. Tap the bottom of the pan on the work surface to get rid of any air bubbles.

8. Bake until a wooden pick inserted in the center comes out clean, 45 to 50 minutes.

9. Cool in the pan on a wire rack for 15 minutes. If necessary, loosen the cake from the sides of the pan with a small knife. Carefully flip the cake upside down onto the wire rack, peel off the parchment paper, and then turn the cake right side up onto the rack to cool completely.

WHITE CAKE

Makes one 9 x 13-inch sheet cake or 24 cupcakes

2 cups all-purpose flour
2 teaspoons baking powder
⅛ teaspoon salt
1 stick (4 ounces) salted butter, at room temperature
¼ cup solid vegetable shortening
1½ cups sugar
2 teaspoons vanilla extract
¼ teaspoon almond extract
5 large egg whites
¾ cup whole milk

1. Preheat the oven to 350°F. Grease a 9 x 13-inch metal baking pan and line the bottom with parchment paper. (Or see the cupcake variation below.)

2. In a medium bowl, whisk together the flour, baking powder, and salt. Set aside.

3. In a large bowl, with an electric mixer, beat the butter and shortening until softened. Add the sugar and beat until light and fluffy, 3 to 5 minutes. Scrape down the sides of the bowl as needed.

4. Beat in the vanilla and almond extracts.

5. Add the egg whites, one at a time, beating well after each addition. Scrape down the sides of the bowl as needed.

6. On low speed, alternate adding the flour mixture and the milk to the butter mixture, beginning and ending with the flour mixture.

7. Pour the batter into the prepared pan and smooth the top with a spatula. Tap the bottom of the pan on the work surface to get rid of any air bubbles.

8. Bake until a wooden pick inserted in the center of the cake comes out clean, 35 to 40 minutes.

9. Cool in the pan on a wire rack for 15 minutes. If necessary, loosen the cake from the sides of the pan with a small knife. Carefully flip the cake upside down onto the wire rack, peel off the parchment paper, and then turn the cake right side up onto the rack to cool completely.

White Cupcakes: Line 24 cups of 2 muffin tins with paper liners and fill two-thirds full with batter. (Or use 1 muffin tin and bake in two batches.) Bake at 350°F until a wooden pick inserted in the center of a cupcake comes out clean, 18 to 20 minutes. Transfer to a wire rack to cool.

RED VELVET CAKE

Makes one 9 x 13-inch sheet cake or 24 cupcakes

2 cups all-purpose flour

¼ cup unsweetened cocoa powder

½ teaspoon baking soda

½ teaspoon salt

1 stick (4 ounces) salted butter, at room temperature

2 cups sugar

3 large eggs

2 teaspoons vanilla extract

1 cup sour cream

½ cup whole milk

1½ tablespoons red food coloring

1. Preheat the oven to 350°F. Grease a 9 x 13-inch metal baking pan. Line the bottom with parchment paper, grease the paper, and flour the pan. (Or see the cupcake variation below.)

2. In a medium bowl, whisk together the flour, cocoa powder, baking soda, and salt.

3. In a large bowl, with an electric mixer, beat the butter until creamy. Add the sugar and beat until light and fluffy, 3 to 5 minutes.

4. In a small bowl, whisk together the eggs and vanilla. In another small bowl, whisk together the sour cream and milk. Pour the egg mixture into the butter-sugar mixture and beat on medium speed for 2 minutes.

5. On low speed, alternate adding the flour mixture and the sour cream mixture to the butter-egg mixture, beginning and ending with the flour adding the food coloring with the first addition of liquid.

6. Pour the batter into the prepared pan and spread evenly. Tap the pan on the work surface to get rid of any air bubbles.

7. Bake until a wooden pick inserted in the center comes out clean, 25 to 28 minutes.

8. Cool in the pan on a wire rack for 15 minutes. If necessary, loosen the sides of the cake with a knife. Carefully flip the cake upside down onto the rack, peel off the parchment paper, and then turn the cake right side up onto the rack to cool completely.

Red Velvet Cupcakes: Line 24 cups of 2 muffin tins with paper liners and fill two-thirds full with batter. (Or use 1 muffin tin and bake in two batches.) Bake at 350°F until a wooden pick inserted in the center of a cupcake comes out clean, 18 to 20 minutes. Transfer to a wire rack to cool.

RICH CHOCOLATE CAKE

Makes one 9 x 13-inch sheet cake or 24 cupcakes

1⅓ cups all-purpose flour

⅔ cup unsweetened cocoa powder, plus more for dusting the pan

1½ teaspoons baking soda

1 teaspoon baking powder

½ teaspoon ground cinnamon

½ teaspoon salt

1⅓ cups granulated sugar

⅔ cup firmly packed light brown sugar

4 large eggs

⅓ cup water

2 teaspoons vanilla extract

1 cup sour cream

¼ cup vegetable oil

1. Preheat the oven to 325°F. Grease a 9 x 13-inch metal baking pan. Line the bottom with parchment paper, grease the paper, and dust the pan with cocoa powder. (Or see the cupcake variation below.)

2. In a large bowl, whisk together the flour, cocoa powder, baking soda, baking powder, cinnamon, and salt. Whisk in both sugars until evenly combined. Set aside.

3. In a medium bowl, whisk together the eggs, water, and vanilla. Whisk in the sour cream and oil.

4. Make a well in the center of the flour mixture and add the sour cream mixture. Stir until no dry streaks of flour remain (do not overmix).

5. Pour the batter into the prepared pan and spread evenly. Tap the pan on the work surface to get rid of any air bubbles.

6. Bake until a wooden pick inserted in the center comes out clean, 35 to 40 minutes.

7. Cool in the pan on a wire rack for 15 minutes. If necessary, loosen the cake from the sides of the pan with a small knife. Carefully flip the cake upside down onto the wire rack, peel off the parchment paper, and then turn the cake right side up onto the rack to cool completely.

Rich Chocolate Cupcakes: Line 24 cups of 2 muffin tins with paper liners and fill each two-thirds full with batter. (Or use 1 muffin tin and bake in two batches.) Bake at 325°F until a wooden pick inserted in the center of a cupcake comes out clean, 18 to 20 minutes. Transfer to a wire rack to cool.

NEW YORK–STYLE CHEESECAKE

Makes one 9-inch round cheesecake

CRUST
1½ cups cookie crumbs (graham crackers, gingersnaps, or chocolate wafers)
¼ cup sugar
5 tablespoons salted butter, melted

FILLING
4 packages (8 ounces each) cream cheese, at room temperature
¾ cup sugar
2 large eggs, lightly beaten
1 teaspoon vanilla extract
2 tablespoons cornstarch
1 cup sour cream

1. Preheat the oven to 350°F.

2. Make the crust: In a large bowl, whisk together the cookie crumbs and sugar. Stir in the melted butter until the crumbs are evenly moistened. Press the crumb mixture onto the bottom and 2 inches up the sides of a 9-inch springform pan. Bake for 10 minutes to set the crust. Remove from the oven to cool, but leave the oven on.

3. Make the filling: In a large bowl, with an electric mixer, beat together the cream cheese and sugar until smooth and light.

4. Beat in the eggs, vanilla, and cornstarch until just combined (do not overmix).

5. Mix in the sour cream until well blended.

6. Pour the mixture into the prepared crust and spread evenly.

7. Bake at 350°F for 45 minutes. Turn the oven off, prop the door open slightly, and let the cake sit for 1 hour.

8. Remove from the oven and place on a wire rack to cool to room temperature.

9. Cover and refrigerate until well chilled before serving. (My trick: I place a dinner plate wrapped in a clean kitchen towel on top of the springform to prevent any condensation from dripping onto the cake.)

SWEET CINNAMON ROLLS

Makes 12 rolls

DOUGH
1 envelope (¼ ounce) active dry yeast
¼ cup warm water (105° to 110°F)
6 tablespoons salted butter, at room temperature
¼ cup granulated sugar
4 large egg yolks
¾ cup whole milk, at room temperature
1 teaspoon ground cardamom
¼ teaspoon salt
3½ to 4 cups all-purpose flour
Vegetable oil, for the bowl

FILLING
⅔ cup firmly packed light brown sugar
1 tablespoon ground cinnamon
4 tablespoons salted butter, melted

VANILLA GLAZE
2¼ cups powdered sugar
1 teaspoon vanilla extract
3 tablespoons whole milk

1. Make the dough: In a small bowl, dissolve the yeast in the warm water. Let stand until foamy, about 5 minutes.

2. In a large bowl, with an electric mixer, beat the butter and granulated sugar until smooth.

3. Add the egg yolks one at a time, beating well after each addition. Mix in the milk, cardamom, and salt until well combined. Beat in the yeast mixture. Add 3½ cups of the flour and mix until well combined.

4. On a lightly floured surface, knead the dough until smooth, adding more flour if necessary.

5. Place the dough into a large oiled bowl and cover with plastic wrap. Let rise until doubled in volume, about 1 hour.

6. Make the filling: In a small bowl, combine the brown sugar and cinnamon.

7. On a lightly floured surface, roll the dough into a 12 x 18-inch rectangle. Brush with the butter and sprinkle with the filling. Starting at a short end, roll the dough into a cylinder. Slice crosswise into 12 equal pieces.

8. Preheat the oven to 350°F. Grease a 9 x 13-inch baking pan. Lay the rolls in the pan. Cover with plastic wrap and let rise until light and puffed, about 30 minutes.

9. Bake until the rolls are golden brown, about 20 minutes. Transfer to a wire rack to cool completely.

10. Make the vanilla glaze: In a small bowl, combine the powdered sugar and vanilla. Slowly whisk in the milk until the mixture has a spreadable consistency. Spread the glaze over the rolls.

BROWNIES

Makes 9 to 16 brownies

1 cup plus 2 tablespoons sugar
½ cup all-purpose flour
⅓ cup unsweetened cocoa powder
¼ teaspoon baking powder
¼ teaspoon salt
½ cup vegetable oil
⅓ cup whole milk
1 teaspoon vanilla extract
1 large egg

1. Preheat the oven to 350°F. Grease an 8 x 8-inch metal baking pan. Line the bottom and two sides of the pan with parchment paper (leave an overhang to make it easier to take out of the pan).

2. In a medium bowl, whisk together the sugar, flour, cocoa powder, baking powder, and salt.

3. Add the oil, milk, vanilla, and egg. Whisk until well combined.

4. Pour the batter into the prepared pan and spread evenly.

5. Bake until a wooden pick inserted in the center comes out mostly clean, 20 to 25 minutes.

6. Let the brownies cool in the pan, then cut into squares before serving.

MACARONS

Makes 24 sandwich cookies

MACARONS
2 cups powdered sugar
1 cup almond meal (Bob's Red Mill)
3 large egg whites, at room temperature
¼ cup granulated sugar
¼ teaspoon salt
Food coloring (optional)

FILLING
4 ounces cream cheese, at room temperature
2 tablespoons salted butter, at room temperature
6 tablespoons powdered sugar
½ teaspoon vanilla extract
Food coloring (optional)

1. Make the macarons: Sift the powdered sugar into a bowl. Repeat this process with the almond meal. Discard any large chunks of almond (you want a very smooth batter). Whisk the powdered sugar and almond meal until combined.

2. In a bowl, with an electric mixer, beat the egg whites until frothy, about 4 minutes. Continue beating, slowing adding the granulated sugar until soft peaks form, about 4 minutes longer. (Do not beat to stiff peaks or you won't get smooth cookies.)

3. Fold in the salt.

4. If using food coloring, mix it in now (use a color a little darker than the color you're looking for, because it will bake up lighter).

5. Using a spatula, gently fold about one-third of the almond mixture into the egg white mixture, about 20 strokes. Repeat this process two more times.

6. Line a baking sheet with parchment paper.

7. Spoon the batter into a decorating bag fitted with either the coupler or a #806 tip. Pipe 1-inch rounds ¾ inch apart on the parchment paper. Tap the baking sheet to release any air bubbles and let sit for 1 hour before baking to develop a "skin."

8. Position a rack in the top third of the oven and preheat the oven to 300°F.

9. Bake the cookies until they have puffed up and look dry (they should not brown), about 20 minutes. They will develop a rough-looking layer called the "foot." Let them cool completely on the pan.

10. Make the filling: In a bowl, with an electric mixer, beat the cream cheese, butter, powdered sugar, and vanilla until smooth and creamy. If using food coloring, mix it in now. Scoop into a decorating bag fitted with a #12 tip.

11. Turn half of the macarons upside down. Pipe about 1 teaspoon of filling onto each. Top with the remaining macarons.

CHOCOLATE CHIP COOKIES

Makes about 3 dozen cookies

2½ cups all-purpose flour
2 teaspoons baking soda
1 teaspoon salt
2 sticks (8 ounces) salted butter, at room
    temperature
¾ cup granulated sugar
¾ cup firmly packed light brown sugar
1 teaspoon vanilla extract
2 large eggs
12 ounces semisweet chocolate chips

1. Preheat the oven to 375°F.

2. In a medium bowl, whisk together the flour, baking soda, and salt.

3. In a large bowl, with an electric mixer, cream together the butter, granulated sugar, brown sugar, and vanilla.

4. Add the eggs, one at a time, beating well after each addition. Scrape down the sides of the bowl as needed.

5. On low speed, beat in the flour mixture until combined.

6. Fold in the chocolate chips.

7. Place 2 tablespoons of dough per cookie onto an ungreased baking sheet, spacing them 2 inches apart.

8. Bake until golden brown, 7 to 9 minutes.

9. Let the cookies cool on the baking sheet for 1 minute, then transfer to a wire rack to cool completely.

CREAM CHEESE SUGAR COOKIES

Makes about 30 cookies

⅔ cup solid vegetable shortening
⅓ cup salted butter, at room temperature
3 ounces cream cheese, at room temperature
¾ cup granulated sugar
1 tablespoon powdered sugar
½ teaspoon salt
1 teaspoon vanilla extract
1 large egg
2 cups all-purpose flour
Food coloring (optional)

1. In a large bowl, with an electric mixer, beat together the shortening, butter, cream cheese, granulated sugar, powdered sugar, salt, vanilla, and egg until light and fluffy.

2. Beat in the flour until blended. Mix in the food coloring (if using).

3. Roll the dough into a log and wrap in plastic wrap. Refrigerate for at least 1 hour to firm up.

4. Preheat the oven to 375°F. Line a baking sheet with parchment paper.

5. Break off pieces of dough (about 2 tablespoons each) and roll into the size of golf balls. Place the balls about 1 inch apart on the baking sheet and lightly press down, flattening the dough to ½ inch thick.

6. Bake until the bottoms are lightly browned, 7 to 9 minutes.

7. Let cool on the baking sheet for 2 minutes, then transfer to a wire rack to cool completely.

VANILLA ALMOND SUGAR COOKIES

Makes 4 dozen cookies

½ cup blanched almonds, or ¾ cup almond meal
1½ cups plus 1 tablespoon sugar
3 cups all-purpose flour
1 teaspoon baking powder
½ teaspoon freshly grated nutmeg
⅛ teaspoon salt
2 sticks (8 ounces) salted butter, at room temperature
2 large eggs
1½ teaspoons vanilla extract
½ teaspoon almond extract

1. In a blender, combine the almonds and 1 tablespoon of the sugar and process until finely ground. (If using almond meal, you can skip this step and just add the sugar when you add the almond meal to the flour.) Transfer to a medium bowl and whisk in the flour, baking powder, nutmeg, and salt. Set aside.

2. In a large bowl, with an electric mixer, beat the butter until softened. Add the remaining 1½ cups sugar and beat until light and fluffy, 3 to 5 minutes. Scrape down the sides of the bowl as needed.

3. Add the eggs, one at a time, beating well after each addition. Scrape down the sides of the bowl as needed.

4. Beat in the vanilla and almond extracts.

5. On low speed, beat in the flour mixture until combined.

6. Shape the dough into 2 disks about 1 inch thick. Wrap the disks in plastic wrap and refrigerate for at least 1 hour and up to overnight.

7. Position the racks in the middle and lower third of the oven and preheat to 350°F. Line 2 baking sheets with parchment paper, or grease and lightly flour.

8. Working with one disk at a time on a lightly floured surface, roll out the dough ¼ inch thick. Cut out cookies using a 2½-inch round cookie cutter and place them 1 inch apart on the baking sheets. (Re-roll the dough scraps and cut out more cookies.)

9. Bake for 12 to 13 minutes, switching the pans from top to bottom and rotating them front to back halfway through. The cookies should be firm to the touch but not browned at the edges.

10. Let cool for 2 minutes on the baking sheets, then transfer to a wire rack to cool completely.

LEMON SUGAR COOKIES

Makes 4 dozen cookies

3 cups all-purpose flour
1 teaspoon baking powder
⅛ teaspoon salt
2 sticks (8 ounces) salted butter, at room temperature
1½ cups sugar
2 large eggs
1½ tablespoons finely grated lemon zest
1 tablespoon lemon juice
1 teaspoon vanilla extract

1. In a medium bowl, whisk together the flour, baking powder, and salt. Set aside.

2. In a large bowl, with an electric mixer, beat the butter until softened. Add the sugar and beat until light and fluffy, 3 to 5 minutes. Scrape down the sides of the bowl as needed.

3. Add the eggs, one at a time, beating well after each addition. Scrape down the sides of the bowl as needed.

4. Beat in the lemon zest, lemon juice, and vanilla.

5. On low speed, beat in the flour mixture until well combined.

6. Shape the dough into 2 disks about 1 inch thick. Wrap the disks in plastic wrap and refrigerate for at least 1 hour and up to overnight.

7. Position the racks in the middle and lower third of the oven and preheat the oven to 350°F. Line 2 baking sheets with parchment paper, or grease and lightly flour.

8. Working with one disk at a time on a lightly floured surface, roll out the dough ¼ inch thick. Cut out cookies using a 2½-inch round cookie cutter and place them 1 inch apart on the baking sheets. (Re-roll the dough scraps to cut out more cookies.)

9. Bake for 12 to 13 minutes, switching the pans from top to bottom and rotating them front to back halfway through. The cookies should be firm to the touch, but not browned at the edges.

10. Let cool for 2 minutes on the baking sheets, then transfer to a wire rack to cool completely.

ROYAL ICING

Makes about 4 cups

Royal icing is perfect for decorating cookies and other treats. It can be colored or flavored easily and dries to a hard, smooth matte finish.

5 egg whites (see Note)
½ teaspoon vanilla extract
4 cups powdered sugar
Lemon juice (optional)

1. In a large bowl, whisk the egg whites and vanilla until frothy.

2. Add the powdered sugar a few tablespoons at a time, mixing after each addition, to reach the desired consistency. (If you want the icing to be really white, add a few drops of lemon juice when mixing the powdered sugar into the egg white mixture.)

NOTE: *You can use powdered egg whites or meringue powder instead of raw egg whites.*

MARSHMALLOW FONDANT

Makes 24 ounces

1 bag (10 ounces) mini marshmallows
3 tablespoons water
6 cups powdered sugar
Oil, for greasing your hands
Food coloring gel (optional)

1. Pour the marshmallows into a microwave-safe bowl. Stir in the water to evenly coat the marshmallows.

2. Microwave for 30 seconds, then stir. Repeat this process two more times, or until the mixture is smooth.

3. Sift 3 cups of the powdered sugar into a large bowl and make a hole in the center.

4. Pour the melted marshmallow mixture onto the powdered sugar.

5. Sift the rest of the powdered sugar on top of the marshmallows.

6. Oil your hands to prevent the marshmallows from sticking to you. Knead in the sugar until you have the consistency of soft taffy and the fondant no longer sticks to your hands. If you are tinting the fondant, add food coloring now and knead until the color is fully incorporated. (Coat your hands with shortening so the colors don't stain them.)

7. If you are not using the fondant right away, store it tightly wrapped or in a plastic bag at room temperature.

APPLE
PI PIE

THIS IS ONE OF MY FAVORITE DESSERTS of all time. I've been baking Pi Pies every year since my first calculus teacher brought one to class. They're a special treat for Pi Day, a global celebration of math that falls annually on March 14—3.14, the mathematical constant. Each year I update my recipe to try to create the ultimate Pi Pie, but this is one of my favorites and I'm excited to share it with you! Math and baking . . . can it get any sweeter?

THE THINGS YOU'LL NEED

Pie Dough (page 22)

3½ pounds Granny Smith apples

⅓ cup granulated sugar

⅓ cup firmly packed light brown sugar

3 tablespoons all-purpose flour

1½ teaspoons ground cinnamon

¼ teaspoon ground cloves

⅛ teaspoon ground allspice

3 tablespoons lemon juice

1½ tablespoons salted butter, cubed

Egg wash: 1 egg beaten with 2 tablespoons water

Large (2-inch) and small (¾-inch) number cookie cutters

9-inch deep-dish pie plate

RO·TIP

IF YOU HAVE EXTRA APPLE SLICES, *you can bake them separately as a snack!*

1. Prepare the pie dough and place it in the refrigerator for at least 1 hour before using.

2. With a sharp straight edge (not serrated) knife, cut the apples vertically, from stem to blossom end (to avoid the core), into even ¼-inch-thick slices Ⓐ.

3. Use the large cookie cutters to cut out a bunch of numbers from the apple slices Ⓑ. Place all the apple cutouts into a large bowl.

4. In a medium bowl, whisk together the granulated sugar, brown sugar, flour, cinnamon, cloves, and allspice. Gently fold the sugar mixture into the bowl of apple cutouts, making sure not to break the numbers. Do this until all the numbers are evenly coated Ⓒ.

5. Add the lemon juice to the mixture and carefully fold again.

6. On a lightly floured surface, roll out half the dough ¼ inch thick and fit it into the pie plate. Trim off the excess dough along the rim of the pie plate and save for decorations.

7. Pour the apple pie filling into the pie plate Ⓓ. Try to make the numbers as level as possible so the top crust will lie flat. Place the cubed butter evenly over the filling.

8. Roll out the second half of the dough to about ¼ inch thick. Cut out a circle the same diameter as your pie plate and place it on top of the pie Ⓔ. Save the excess dough for decorations.

9. Preheat the oven to 425°F.

~~~~~~~~~~ TIME TO DECORATE! ~~~~~~~~~~

1. Crimp the edges of the dough with your fingers to make a decorative trim.

2. Brush the egg wash over the pie. This helps the crust turn a nice golden brown and acts as an adhesive for your decorative numbers and pi symbol.

3. Roll out the excess dough and use the small cookie cutters to make the numbers of pi (3.14159265358979323846264 . . .). Mold a pi symbol for the middle of the pie.

4. Place the pi symbol in the middle of the pie. Carefully place the dough numbers around the pie (just inside the crimped border) in the order of pi Ⓕ.

5. Cover the top of the pie with aluminum foil so the crust doesn't brown too quickly. Bake at 425°F for 15 minutes, then reduce the heat to 350°F and bake for 20 minutes more. Remove the foil and bake until golden brown, about 10 minutes more.

6. Let the pie cool before serving.

CHEMISTRY LAB
CAKE

·

THEY SAY CHEMISTS MAKE THE BEST bakers. That's because baking *is* chemistry! Even before you put batter in the oven, several chemical exchanges occur that begin to transform the liquid mixture into a solid cake. Gluten networks form as you mix the batter, while carbon dioxide escaping from baking soda helps the cake rise as it heats. Baking is a science, and there's no better way to honor that science than with this tasty chemistry-themed cake.

THE THINGS YOU'LL NEED

Butter, for greasing the bowls

Pound Cake batter (page 24)

2 tubs (16 ounces each) buttercream frosting

5 cereal treats (Rice Krispies Treats; 0.78 ounce each)

Sky blue food coloring gel

Two 1-quart ovenproof glass bowls (Pyrex)

Cake leveler

8-inch wooden skewer

2 decorating bags

#5 decorating tip

#2 decorating tip

RO TIP

ALWAYS LET YOUR CAKES COOL COMPLETELY *before decorating so they don't crumble, fall apart, or melt your frosting.*

1. Preheat the oven to 330°F. Grease the ovenproof bowls.

2. Prepare the Pound Cake batter.

3. Divide the batter evenly between the bowls and bake until a wooden pick inserted into the center of a cake comes out clean, about 20 minutes.

4. Let the cakes cool in the bowls.

5. Once the cakes are completely cool, remove them from the bowls by turning the bowls upside down over a clean surface. I give mine a few firm shakes.

~~~~~~~~~~ **TIME TO DECORATE!** ~~~~~~~~~~

1. First we are going to make the bottom of the flask. Start by leveling the flat side of both cakes with a large knife to create two flat surfaces.

2. Spread a layer of buttercream frosting over the leveled side of one cake. Place the second cake upside down on top to make a sphere Ⓐ.

3. To make the neck of the flask, press 4 Rice Krispies Treats together and roll them into a cylinder Ⓑ.

4. Roll a small piece of another Rice Krispies Treat into a thin rope and wrap it around one end of the cylinder to make the flask lip Ⓒ. Cut off any excess.

5. Press the pointy end of a wooden skewer 3 to 4 inches into the center of the Rice Krispies Treats cylinder. Insert the other end of the skewer into the middle of the cake, so that the cylinder is centered and standing up straight Ⓓ.

6. Frosting time! Evenly spread buttercream frosting over the entire cake and the neck of the flask Ⓔ.

7. Once the cake is completely frosted, place it in the freezer for 10 minutes to chill.

8. Tint 1 tub of buttercream frosting with sky blue food coloring until you reach the desired shade of light blue. Place the light blue frosting in a decorating bag fitted with a #5 tip.

9. Frost the bottom half of the flask base with the light blue frosting and smooth it out with a spatula Ⓕ.

10. Scoop a small amount of white buttercream frosting into a decorating bag fitted with a #2 tip. Frost milliliter measurements on the flask for detail.

ATOM
COOKIES

ATOMS ARE THE BUILDING BLOCKS of every type of matter in the universe—even you! My grandfather was a nuclear physicist, my uncle followed in his footsteps, and my dad's old high school even had an atom on its emblem. I guess you could say we have an *atomic bond*. I decorated my atoms green, blue, and purple, but you can make your atom cookies any color you want. Just remember: Never trust an atom . . . they make up everything!

THE THINGS YOU'LL NEED

Vanilla Almond Sugar Cookie dough (page 34)

Royal Icing (page 36)

Food coloring gels: black, purple, sky blue, and leaf green

Decorative silver candy pearls

Candy-coated chocolates (M&M's)

Baking sheet

Atom-shaped cookie cutter (template on page 252 or QR code on page 50)

4 decorating bags

#2 decorating tips

RO·TIP YOU CAN USE BAKING TWEEZERS FOR *more accuracy when placing small candies on the treats.*

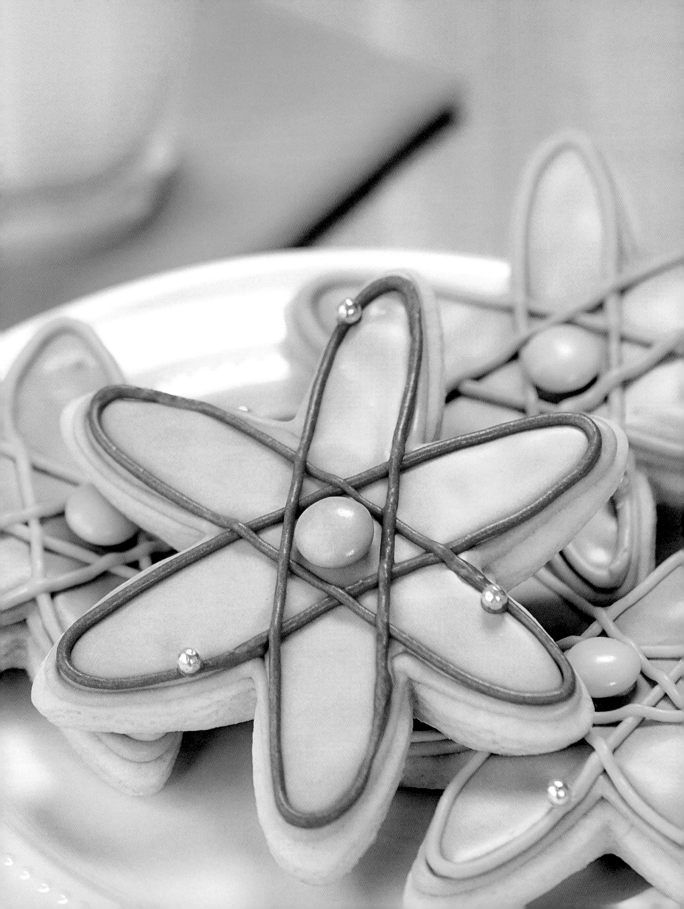

LET'S GET STARTED!

1. Preheat the oven to 350°F. Line a baking sheet with parchment paper.

2. Prepare the Vanilla Almond Sugar Cookie dough.

3. On a lightly floured surface, roll out the dough ¼ inch thick Ⓐ.

4. Cut out cookies using the atom cookie cutter Ⓑ, re-rolling the scraps to get as many cookies as you can. (If you don't have an atom cookie cutter, use the template on page 252 or the QR code to make a stencil.)

5. Place the cookies 1 inch apart on the baking sheet Ⓒ.

6. Bake until golden brown, 7 to 9 minutes.

7. Let the cookies cool on the baking sheet for 2 minutes, then transfer to a wire rack to cool completely.

SCAN
for Atom
Cookie
Template

TIME TO DECORATE!

1. While the cookies are cooling, make the Royal Icing. For gray, mix in black food coloring one drop at a time until you reach the desired shade of gray. Make three other icing colors of your choosing. I chose purple, sky blue, and leaf green to match the candies I was using.

2. Scoop the gray icing into a decorating bag fitted with a #2 tip, and outline the atom cookies Ⓓ.

3. Once the outline hardens, fill the center with more gray icing. You can use a toothpick to help spread it evenly Ⓔ.

4. Now it's time for the colored icings! Scoop the colored icings into decorating bags fitted with #2 tips, and pipe on the colored electron rings.

5. Add candy pearls to the electron rings (one per ring) while the icing is still wet. Pipe a dab of icing on the bottom of the M&M's and carefully place one in the middle of each atom Ⓕ.

PERIODIC TABLE
OF CUPCAKES

SPEAKING OF ATOMS, EVERY TYPE IS DIFFERENT. These types are called elements, and scientists can see how they interact with one another by using the periodic table. Some are solid, like iron and gold, and others are gases, such as neon and helium. Certain kinds have aspects of both solids and gases, but all of them will taste great when they're served at your periodic *kitchen* table. Get it? You can have that one. On the house.

THE THINGS YOU'LL NEED

- **5 batches White Cake batter (page 25); see step 2**
- **12 tubs (16 ounces each) buttercream frosting**
- **Food coloring gels: electric pink, sky blue, electric yellow, electric orange, leaf green, electric green, purple, royal blue, red, and black**
- **5 bags (12 ounces each) white Candy Melts (Wilton) or white chocolate**
- **Royal Icing (page 36)**

- **Muffin tin(s)**
- **Brown cupcake liners**
- **12 decorating bags**
- **Wilton silicone 24-cavity "Brownie Square" mold**
- **#807 decorating tip**
- **#2 decorating tip**
- **#1 decorating tip**

RO TIP

YOU CAN PLACE YOUR FILLED *silicone mold in the fridge to help the white candy set faster.*

1. Preheat the oven to 350°F. Line 12 cups of a muffin tin with brown paper liners.

2. Prepare the White Cake batter. You need enough batter to make 118 cupcakes (for the 118 elements on the periodic table). I like to make each batch separately.

3. Fill each muffin cup two-thirds full with batter. Bake until a wooden pick inserted in the center of a cupcake comes out clean, 18 to 20 minutes. Repeat for all batches.

4. Let the cupcakes cool completely on a wire rack before decorating.

5. The list below shows the periodic table families and the number of cupcakes you will need for each. The colors I chose to dye the frosting are in parentheses, but you can pick whatever colors you'd like Ⓐ. Use 1 tub for each color and 2 tubs for the Transition Metals. (There is an extra tub as a backup, in case you heavily frost your cupcakes.)

6 Alkaline Earth Metals (Gray)

6 Alkali Metals (Red)

6 Halogens (Electric Green)

7 Metalloids (Electric Orange)

7 Noble Gases (Leaf Green)

7 Other Nonmetals (Electric Yellow)

11 Post-Transition Metals (Electric Pink)

15 Actinoids (Royal Blue)

15 Lanthanoids (Sky Blue)

38 Transition Metals (Purple)

～～～～～ TIME TO DECORATE! ～～～～～

1. Using decorating bags fitted with a #807 tip, frost all the cupcakes with their respective colors Ⓑ.

2. In the microwave or a double boiler, melt the white Candy Melts. Pipe about ¼ inch into the cups of the silicone mold Ⓒ. (I use a decorating bag fitted with a #2 tip for more control.) Let cool for 10 minutes.

3. When the white candy squares have hardened, pop them out Ⓓ. Repeat the process until you have 118 squares.

4. Make the Royal Icing. Mix black food coloring into the icing until it is solid black. Scoop the icing into a decorating bag fitted with a #2 tip and pipe the element abbreviations onto your squares Ⓔ. Switch the tip on the decorating bag to a #1 tip and write the element numbers in the upper right-hand corners with black icing.

5. Place the squares onto the centers of your frosted cupcakes, organizing them by the family colors you chose Ⓕ. Arrange your finished cupcakes into the periodic table!

PETRI DISH
JELLIES

My MOM working in the lab (don't mind the elephant costume, it was Halloween).

MY MOM WAS A MEDICAL TECHNICIAN for over a decade and spent a lot of that time looking at Petri dishes through a microscope. Sometimes I like to set up my own Petri dishes, but mine are a lot more edible than what she was working with. You can create all kinds of tasty cultures with different gelatins and gummies—just remember to take a peek when you're done. You can really see the flavor!

THE THINGS YOU'LL NEED

5 boxes (3 ounces each) gelatin (Jell-O), one of each flavor: lime, lemon, orange, berry blue, and cherry lemonade

Assorted gummy candies: gummy raspberries (Trolli), gummy octopus (Trolli), sour candy rope (Haribo), gummy worms, and gummy frogs (Haribo)

Heatproof medium bowl (Pyrex)

Baster

Several Petri dishes

RO TIP

USE ANY OF YOUR FAVORITE GUMMY CANDIES *to look like germs or bacteria! (Trim them to bacteria-like shapes if necessary.)*

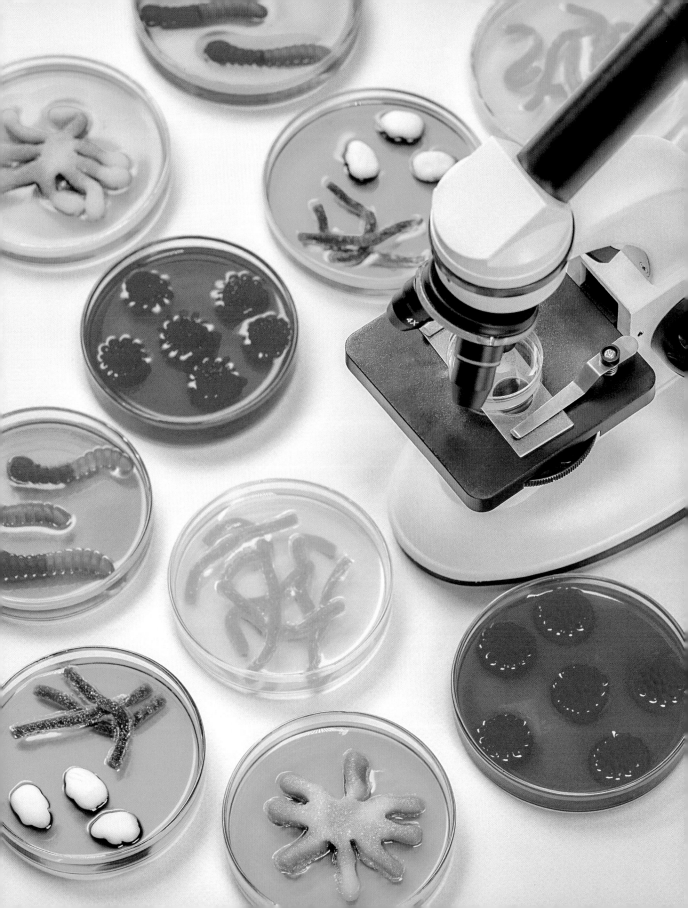

1. Work with one flavor of Jell-O at a time. In a saucepan, bring 1 cup water to a boil Ⓐ.

2. Empty a packet of Jell-O in a heatproof medium bowl and add the boiling water Ⓑ, whisking until completely dissolved, about 3 minutes.

3. Once the gelatin powder is dissolved, add 1 cup cold water and whisk again Ⓒ.

4. Use a baster to add the liquid gelatin mixture to the Petri dishes, filling them two-thirds full Ⓓ. The amount of Jell-O you've made will fill several Petri dishes. If you don't use all of the Jell-O, just pour it into a tray to make extra snacks.

5. Repeat steps 1 through 4 for each gelatin flavor you are using.

6. Let the Petri dishes chill in the refrigerator until the Jello-O is partially set (slightly liquid), about 1 hour.

1. While the Jell-O is in the fridge, prepare the candies to look like bacterial cultures Ⓔ. Get creative with it!

2. After 1 hour, place the candies in the Petri dishes to look like different germs and bacteria Ⓕ.

3. Chill the Petri dishes in the refrigerator until set, about 1 hour 30 minutes.

RED BLOOD CELL
CUPCAKES

RED BLOOD CELLS ARE CALLED ERYTHROCYTES, and their job is to deliver oxygen from the lungs to the rest of the body. A molecule called hemoglobin gives them their distinctive red color. It's also the reason blood is red! You aren't normally supposed to mount blood cells thousands of times their original size onto red velvet cupcakes and eat them, but it's a great way to gross out your friends and impress any big cytology buffs in the family.

∼ THE THINGS YOU'LL NEED ∼

Red Velvet Cake batter (page 26)

About 66 red fruit chews (Starburst Fruit Punch)

½ tub (8 ounces) buttercream frosting

Red food coloring gel

1¾ cups water

⅓ cup sugar

2 cups raspberries

2 tablespoons cornstarch

Muffin tin(s)

Brown cupcake liners

Fine-mesh sieve

RO TIP

IF YOU'RE IN A HURRY, YOU CAN *skip the puree and use red buttercream frosting to decorate.*

1. Preheat the oven to 350°F. Line 24 muffin cups of 2 muffin tins with brown paper liners. (Or use 1 muffin tin and bake in batches.)

2. Prepare the Red Velvet Cake batter. Fill each muffin cup two-thirds full with batter.

3. Bake until a wooden pick inserted into the center of a cupcake comes out clean, 18 to 20 minutes.

4. Let the cupcakes cool completely before decorating.

1. Cut the Starbursts into quarters. Roll the quarters into little balls and indent them in the middle to look like blood cells. I use a circular fondant-shaping tool Ⓐ.

2. Tint the buttercream frosting with red food coloring until you reach the desired shade of red.

3. Position the "red blood cells" on top of the cupcakes, using a dab of red buttercream frosting as an adhesive Ⓑ.

4. In a saucepan, combine the water, sugar, and raspberries Ⓒ. Bring to a boil, then reduce the heat and let simmer for 30 minutes.

5. Set a fine-mesh sieve over a measuring cup and pour the raspberry mixture into the sieve. Use a wooden spoon to gently mash the mixture through the sieve to separate the seeds Ⓓ. Discard the seeds.

6. Return the raspberry puree to the saucepan Ⓔ. Gradually stir the cornstarch into the mixture and bring to a boil over medium heat, stirring constantly until the mixture thickens. Remove the saucepan from the heat and let cool.

7. Drizzle the raspberry sauce over the blood cells on the cupcakes. I use a plastic medical syringe Ⓕ for accuracy, and to gross out my friends.

VOLCANO CAKE

WHAT'S BETTER THAN A CAKE SHAPED like a volcano? How about a working volcano that's also a cake! When living in Hawaii, I hiked through miles of lava caverns and igneous rock trails to see rivers of active lava flowing across the island, and this cake belches smoke just like the real thing! Unlike the real thing, there's also an unsuspecting dino wandering around this volcanic treat. Maybe someone should warn him? Oh well. He'll be fine . . . probably.

~ THE THINGS YOU'LL NEED ~

Butter, for greasing the pans

3 batches Rich Chocolate Cake batter (page 27); see step 2

1 tub (16 ounces) chocolate frosting

3 tubs (16 ounces each) buttercream frosting

Food coloring gels: ivory, sky blue, royal blue, and leaf green

1 box (about 14 ounces) graham crackers (Honey Maid)

Green fondant

Small pretzel sticks (Snyder's)

Marshmallow Fondant (page 37), tinted gray (optional)

Four 6-inch round cake pans

One 8-inch round cake pan

Cake leveler

16-ounce plastic water bottle

2 decorating bags

#22 decorating tip

#233 decorating tip

Silicone leaf mold (Wilton)

Dry ice

RO TIP

BE VERY CAREFUL USING DRY ICE. *It should not touch your skin!*

1. Preheat the oven to 350°F. Grease four 6-inch round cake pans and one 8-inch round cake pan. (Work in batches if you don't have four 6-inch pans.)

2. Prepare 3 batches of the Rich Chocolate Cake batter.

3. Divide the batter among the five prepared cake pans. Bake the cakes until a wooden pick inserted in the center of the cake comes out clean, 30 to 35 minutes.

4. Remove the cakes from the pans while they are still warm but not hot, and transfer to a wire rack to cool completely.

5. Once the cakes are fully cooled, level them with a cake leveler or large knife.

6. Place a water bottle on the center of one 6-inch cake and cut around the water bottle with a knife. Remove the center of the cake. Repeat for the rest of the 6-inch cakes A.

7. Cut off the top of the water bottle B.

8. Place the water bottle into the center of one 6-inch cake. Frost the cake with chocolate frosting and then stack the other 6-inch cakes on top, frosting between them C.

9. Place the stacked 6-inch cakes into the freezer for 30 minutes to chill. The colder your cake is, the better for carving.

10. Using a sharp straight edge (not serrated) knife, carve the cakes into the shape of a volcano D.

11. Set the 8-inch cake layer on a cake plate or cake board. Transfer the volcano to the 8-inch cake layer. I use a cake lifter to help move the cakes E.

12. Frost the volcano using chocolate frosting F.

1. Tint 1 tub of the buttercream frosting with ivory food coloring until you reach the desired shade of tan.

2. Frost the 8-inch round cake with the tan frosting.

3. Using a blender or your hands, finely crush the graham crackers to look like sand.

4. Sprinkle the graham cracker crumbs onto the tan frosting to look like a beach G.

5. Tint half a tub of buttercream frosting with sky blue food coloring until you reach the desired shade of light blue. Tint the second half tub of buttercream frosting with royal blue food coloring until you reach the desired shade of dark blue.

6. Carefully scoop the frostings separately into a decorating bag fitted with a #22 tip, trying not to let the frosting colors mix. Pipe waves along the base of the cake H.

7. Tint the remaining 1 tub of buttercream frosting with leaf green food coloring until you reach the desired shade of green. Scoop it into a decorating bag fitted with a #233 tip and pipe the green grass along the base and sides of the volcano I.

8. Make small leaves by pressing green fondant into a silicone leaf mold. Press 3 leaves on top of each pretzel stick to make a tree J. Insert the trees into the "sand" at the base of the volcano.

9. If you'd like, use gray and green fondant to mold a small dinosaur and place him near the base of the volcano K.

10. To create the erupting effect of a volcano, use tongs and gloves to carefully drop small pieces of dry ice into the water bottle in the center of the cake. Pour warm water into the water bottle and watch the eruption happen L!

DINOSAUR FOSSIL
CAKE

WHY DIDN'T ANYONE WARN HIM?! At least he makes a handsome fossil. The preserved remains of prehistoric plants and animals, fossils occur when an organism is covered by rock and left undisturbed for millions of years, leaving an intact skeleton or imprint for paleontologists to study. That's how we know about dinosaurs like our friend here, whose bones just happened to have been made of white chocolate. May he be as delicious as he was in life. Rest in cake.

THE THINGS YOU'LL NEED

Butter, for greasing the pans

Rich Chocolate Cake batter (page 27)

1 tub (16 ounces) chocolate frosting

1 package (about 14 ounces) chocolate sandwich cookies (Oreos)

1 box (about 14 ounces) graham crackers (Honey Maid)

2 bags (12 ounces each) white Candy Melts (Wilton) or white chocolate

Two 8-inch round cake pans

Cake leveler

Decorating bag

#2 decorating tip

Silicone dinosaur skeleton ice cube mold (Fred & Friends)

1. Preheat the oven to 350°F. Grease two 8-inch round cake pans.

2. Prepare the Rich Chocolate Cake batter.

3. Divide the batter between the prepared pans and bake until a wooden pick inserted in the center comes out clean, 30 to 35 minutes.

4. Let the cakes cool in the pans for 10 minutes. When the cakes are warm but not hot, remove them from the pans and place the cakes on a wire rack to cool completely.

5. Level off the tops with a cake leveler or large knife A.

6. Top one layer with chocolate frosting and set the second layer on top of it B.

7. Frost the entire cake with chocolate frosting C.

1. Twist the Oreos apart and scrape off the filling. Using a blender or your hands, finely crush the chocolate cookies and graham crackers. Mix the crumbs together to look like dirt D.

2. In the microwave or a double boiler, melt the white Candy Melts or white chocolate. Using a decorating bag fitted with a #2 tip, pipe the melted candy into the dinosaur skeleton mold E.

3. Let the mold set for 20 minutes, and then pop the pieces out and place them on the top and sides of the cake. The frosting will act as an adhesive and keep the bones in place.

4. Sprinkle the cookie crumb dirt mixture between the bones to cover the entire cake F.

GEODE CANDY
CUPCAKES

THINK THESE ARE ALL ROCKS? THINK AGAIN. As a former rock collector (Nerd alert! We've got a nerd factor five in the building), I can say that some of my favorite mineral formations are geodes. Just about everyone has seen geodes, but do you know they're made when pockets of gas are trapped inside of rock? Minerals form into the shapes of crystals along the interior, creating the solid structures you can crack open and look into! Geodes come in many colors and formations, so you can really get creative with these convincing snacks. See? Rocks are cool!

~ THE THINGS YOU'LL NEED ~

White fondant

Chocolate fondant

3 cups sugar

1 cup water

Purple liquid food coloring

White Cake batter (page 25)

1 tub (16 ounces) buttercream frosting

Assorted colors of hard candies (Jolly Ranchers)

Purple sanding sugar

Small glass bowls

Muffin tins

Brown cupcake liners

RO TIP

IF YOU'RE IN A HURRY, YOU CAN USE *rock candy instead of making the geodes.*

1. To make a geode, roll out the white and chocolate fondant into ⅛-inch-thick rounds about 5 inches across, making the chocolate one a little bigger Ⓐ. Repeat this for a second geode (you can make more geodes if you'd like, as you will have leftover fondant and sugar syrup).

2. For each geode, line a small bowl with several layers of aluminum foil, crumpling the foil unevenly on the inside to make a unique rock-shaped shell Ⓑ.

3. Cover the aluminum foil with the chocolate fondant. Lay the white fondant on top of the chocolate Ⓒ.

4. In a medium saucepan, combine the sugar and water. Whisk constantly over low heat until all the sugar is dissolved. Add 4 drops of purple food coloring Ⓓ. Whisk until the color is completely blended, and remove from the heat.

5. Spoon the purple sugar syrup into the fondant cups until almost full Ⓔ.

6. Completely cover your geodes with aluminum foil Ⓕ and let sit for at least 12 hours, giving the sugar time to crystallize.

7. Take your geodes out of the foil enclosure. Over a bowl, puncture the center of the purple sugar with a sharp knife. Allow the liquid to drip out into the bowl and then carefully scrape out the excess sugar (G).

8. Prop the geodes, crystal side down, over a bowl for at least 2 hours to let the excess liquid drip out and the sugar crystals to dry (H). I place them on top of lollipop sticks for this step.

9. Once the sugar in the center of the geodes is dry, trim off the excess fondant around the edges with a knife (I).

10. Preheat the oven to 350°F. Line 24 cups of 2 muffin tins with brown paper liners. (Or use 1 muffin tin and bake in batches.)

11. Prepare the White Cake batter. Fill each muffin cup two-thirds full with batter.

12. Bake until a wooden pick inserted in the center of a cupcake comes out clean, 18 to 20 minutes.

13. Let the cupcakes cool completely before decorating.

TIME TO DECORATE!

1. Frost the cupcakes with buttercream frosting.

2. Place the hard candies in plastic bags, dividing them by color. Use a hammer or rolling pin to crush the candies so you have large and small pieces (J).

3. Set aside 4 of the cupcakes. Over the remaining cupcakes, sprinkle the smaller pieces of hard candy all over the tops. Place the larger pieces of the hard candies in the center of the cupcakes to make crystal formations (K).

4. Dip the 4 reserved cupcakes in the purple sanding sugar. Carefully cut the geodes in half and place one half in the center of each cupcake (L).

CHAPTER TWO

·SPACE·

STAR CONSTELLATION
COOKIES

ON THE SUMMIT OF HAWAII'S MAUNA KEA, I used to spend time looking at the stars through powerful telescopes. It was easy to fall in love with the gorgeous night sky and its many constellations. The three you see here are the mythical queen Cassiopeia, Ursa Minor (the "little bear," aka the Little Dipper), and Aquila, the eagle of Zeus in Greek mythology. Feeling creative? Re-create your favorite constellations using these star cookies, or design a unique star chart all your own!

THE THINGS YOU'LL NEED

Lemon Sugar Cookie dough (page 35)

Royal Icing (page 36)

Lemon extract or water

White pearl dust (Wilton)

Baking sheet

1-inch star cookie cutter (template on page 252 or QR code on page 86)

Decorating bag

#1 decorating tip

RO·TIP — **KEEP A CLOSE EYE** *on these star cookies as they bake. They will brown quickly due to their small size.*

LET'S GET STARTED!

1. Preheat the oven to 350°F. Line a baking sheet with parchment paper.

2. Prepare the Lemon Sugar Cookie dough.

3. On a lightly floured surface, roll out the dough ¼ inch thick (A).

4. Cut out cookies using the star cookie cutter (B). (If you don't have a star cookie cutter, use the template on page 252 or the QR code to make a stencil.)

5. Place your stars on the lined baking sheet (C) and bake until they are firm to the touch but not browned at the edges, 12 to 13 minutes.

6. Let the cookies cool on the baking sheet for 2 minutes, then transfer to a wire rack to cool completely.

SCAN
for Star
Cookie
Template

TIME TO DECORATE!

1. Make the Royal Icing. Scoop the icing into a decorating bag fitted with a #1 tip, and outline the cookies (D).

2. Fill the center of the cookies with icing. You can use a toothpick to help spread it evenly (E).

3. In a small bowl, mix equal parts lemon extract (or water) and pearl dust. Use the small paintbrush to apply pearl dust to the cookies (F).

4. Arrange the stars into your favorite constellations!

STAR CONSTELLATIONS

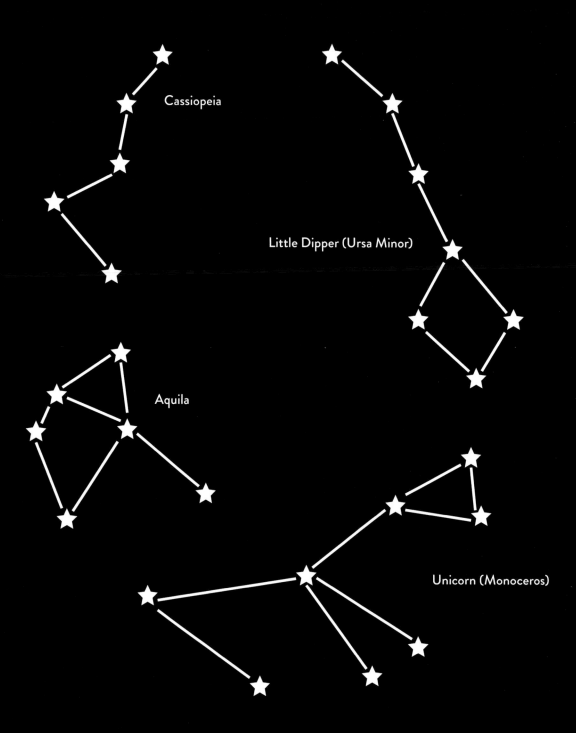

Cassiopeia

Little Dipper (Ursa Minor)

Aquila

Unicorn (Monoceros)

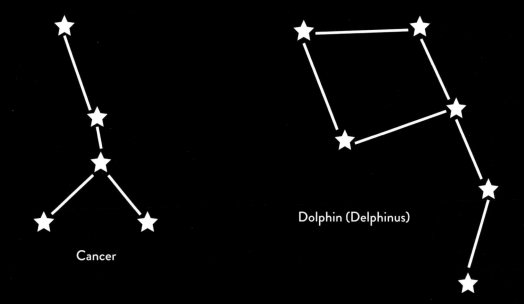

Cancer

Dolphin (Delphinus)

Libra

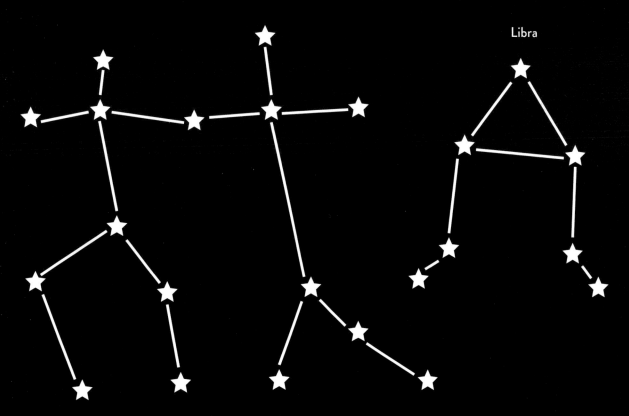

Gemini

MOON CAKE

THE MOON IS EARTH'S ORIGINAL SATELLITE. It orbits our little home, reflecting the light of the sun and the shadow of Earth in what are called lunar phases. Some people say that the moon is made of cheese, but I've always thought it was something sweeter. Cake, maybe? Looks like an astronaut even traveled there to grab a bite!

THE THINGS YOU'LL NEED

Butter, for greasing the bowl

White Cake batter (page 25)

1 tub (16 ounces) buttercream frosting

Black food coloring gel

2½-quart ovenproof glass bowl (Pyrex)

Cake tester

10-inch cardboard cake board

Ice cream scoops (various sizes)

Miniature astronaut figurine (optional decoration)

Miniature flag (optional decoration)

 **RO TIP** WHEN BAKING A CAKE IN A DEEP BOWL, *slow-baking prevents the outside from burning before the center is baked through.*

LET'S GET STARTED!

1. Preheat the oven to 350°F. Grease a 2½-quart ovenproof glass bowl.

2. Prepare the White Cake batter.

3. Pour the batter into the glass bowl **A**.

4. Bake for 15 minutes. Reduce the oven temperature to 300°F and slow-bake until a cake tester inserted in the center comes out clean, about 40 minutes **B**.

5. Let the cake cool and then remove it from the bowl. Level the top with a large knife **C** or cake leveler and place the cake, flat side down, on a cake board.

6. Place the cake in the freezer to chill, about 30 minutes. (This will prevent the cake from crumbling when you decorate.)

TIME TO DECORATE!

1. Using different sizes of ice cream scoops, scoop out pieces of the cake to create moon craters **D**.

2. Tint the buttercream frosting with black food coloring until you reach the desired shade of gray **E**.

3. Frost the moon cake, carefully filling the insides of the craters **F**. Leave some texture in the frosting to make the cake resemble the surface of the moon.

4. Optional: Add an astronaut figurine and flag on top for fun!

MOON PHASE
MACARONS

·

REMEMBER THE LUNAR PHASES? THEY'RE DIVIDED by how the sun casts light across the moon and are described as new, crescent, quarter, gibbous, or full. For a lot of people, my mom included, these phases hold a special significance because of their beauty and meaning—so don't say you're going to eat them! Or do, but break the news gently. Don't want to *eclipse* their feelings.

THE THINGS YOU'LL NEED

Macaron batter and filling (page 31)

Food coloring gels: black, gold, and yellow

Royal Icing (page 36)

Baking sheet

3 decorating bags

#806 decorating tip or coupler

#12 decorating tip

#2 decorating tip

RO·TIP· IF YOU OVERMIX THE BATTER, THE MACARONS *will come out flat. If you undermix, the macarons may puff up or crack.*

LET'S GET STARTED!

1. Prepare the Macaron batter, mixing black food coloring into the meringue mixture in step 4 (before folding in the almond mixture). Make sure you make the batter a deep black because macarons lighten when baked.

2. Trace 1½-inch circles about 1 inch apart on a sheet of parchment paper. Flip the parchment paper over so the tracing is on the underside, and use the paper to line a baking sheet.

3. Scoop the batter into a decorating bag fitted with a coupler (no tip) or a #806 tip. Pipe the macaron batter inside the circle outlines .

4. Let the batter rest for 1 hour and then bake as directed in the macaron recipe (page 31, steps 8 and 9). Let the macarons cool completely on the baking sheet while you make the filling.

5. After making the filling, mix gold and yellow food coloring into the mixture until you get the desired color (I use a ratio of 2 drops gold to 1 drop yellow). Scoop the mixture into a decorating bag fitted with a #12 tip.

6. Flip half of your macarons over and pipe the filling onto the flat bottom .

7. Top with the second half of your macarons .

TIME TO DECORATE!

1. Make the Royal Icing. Mix in gold and yellow food coloring until it matches the color of the macaron filling (I use a ratio of 2 drops gold to 1 drop yellow).

2. Scoop the yellow icing into a decorating bag fitted with a #2 tip and pipe on the outlines of the lunar phases :

1	2	3	4	5	6	7	8
New Moon	Waxing Crescent	First Quarter	Waxing Gibbous	Full Moon	Waning Gibbous	Last Quarter	Waning Crescent

3. Once the outline hardens, fill the centers with icing . You can use a toothpick to help spread it evenly.

EARTH
CAKE

•

I CREATED THIS CAKE ON MY SHOW in celebration of Earth Day! When you cut into it, you can see all the basic layers, from a cake ball core to a frosted crust. The real Earth's inner and outer core are made of metal, a lot less edible than the cake here. These are covered by the mantle—a dense layer of semisolid rock that sometimes shoots out of the surface through volcanoes. That fluid cools and becomes the crust.

THE THINGS YOU'LL NEED

½ batch White Cake batter (page 25)

2 batches Butter Cake batter (page 23)

Food coloring gels: electric yellow, red, sky blue, and leaf green

Shortening, for greasing the pans

2 tubs (16 ounces each) buttercream frosting

Cake Pop Maker (Babycakes)

6-cavity half-sphere (3-inch) silicone mold (Freshware)

6-inch 3-D "Sports Ball" pan set (Wilton)

Decorating bag

#1 decorating tip

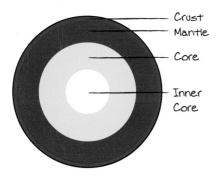

Crust
Mantle

Core

Inner
Core

USE A GLOBE AS A REFERENCE
when piping on the continents.

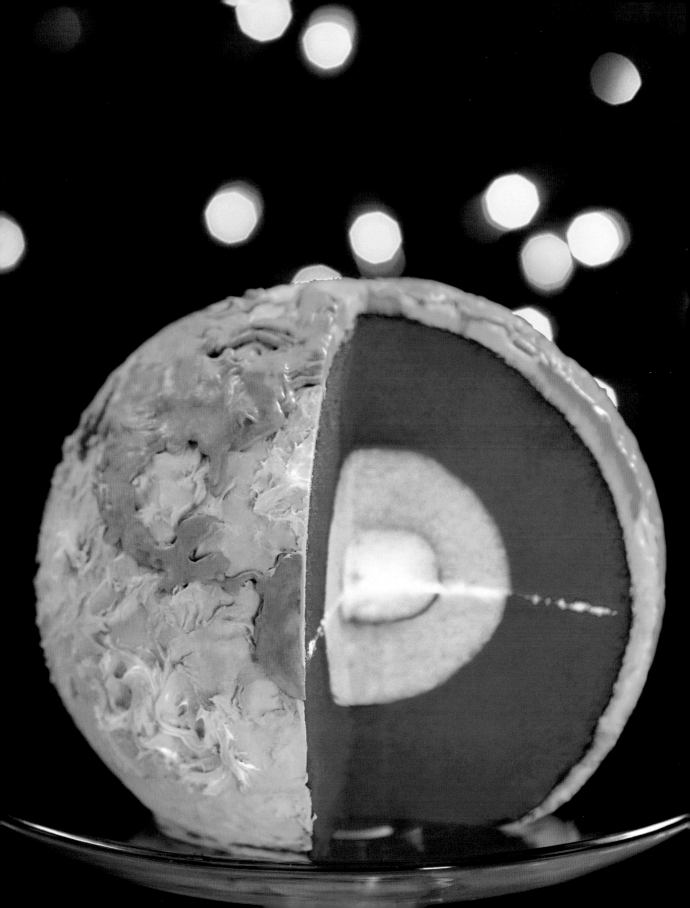

1. Preheat the oven to 350°F.

2. Prepare the White Cake batter and use the batter to make 6 cake balls in an electric cake pop baker.

3. Prepare two batches of the Butter Cake batter and divide it between 2 bowls. Tint one bowl yellow and the other bowl red.

4. Grease the 5 silicone mold cavities and fill with the yellow cake batter. Place a cake ball in the center of each cavity (A). (You only need 2, but I like to make a few extras for backup.)

5. Bake until a wooden pick inserted in the center of the yellow cake comes out clean, 25 to 30 minutes. Let cool completely in the silicone mold.

6. Pop the half-sphere cakes out and trim the edges with a knife to make them completely round and smooth (B).

7. Grease the 6-inch 3-D cake pans with shortening and fill three-quarters full with the red batter. Scoop the batter out of the center of one of the red cakes and quickly place a yellow half-sphere cake in the center. Lightly push the yellow cake down and cover with about ⅛ inch of red batter. Repeat with the second red cake and yellow half-sphere.

8. Bake the cakes until a wooden pick inserted in the center of the red batter comes out clean, 45 minutes to 1 hour. Let the cakes cool in the pans.

9. Remove the cakes from the pans and level with a large knife (C). Flip one cake flat side down and cut a small slice off the rounded side. This will be the bottom of the "Earth," and it needs to stand securely.

10. Flip the bottom of the Earth leveled side up and top it with a thin layer of white frosting. Place the second leveled cake on top to form a sphere (D).

TIME TO DECORATE!

1. Tint 1 tub of buttercream frosting sky blue. Tint the second tub leaf green. Save a little white frosting for cloud details.

2. Place the cake on a cake plate. Spread the blue frosting over the entire cake using a spatula (E). For extra detail, use the spatula to dab the blue frosting to make wave effects in the oceans.

3. Scoop the green frosting into a decorating bag fitted with a #1 tip. Pipe the continents of the world onto your globe (F). Use a spatula to dab little spots of white frosting all over the globe to look like clouds.

ROCKET SHIP
COOKIE POPS

ROCKET SHIPS HAVE FUELED THE IMAGINATIONS of artists and scientists for decades. This collective curiosity led to more people than ever wondering when humankind would travel to the stars. Cookie pops are a really fun way to send your cookies into orbit, great for parties or birthday treats. So buckle up and blast off into outer taste!

THE THINGS YOU'LL NEED

Vanilla Almond Sugar Cookie dough (page 34)

Royal Icing (page 36)

Food coloring gels: red, yellow, sky blue, and black

Baking sheet

Rocket ship cookie cutter (template on page 252 or QR code on page 104)

Lollipop sticks

5 decorating bags

Five #1 decorating tips

WHEN MAKING LOLLIPOP COOKIES, AVOID *pressing the sticks more than halfway into the cookie dough. They may poke through the front after baking.*

LET'S GET STARTED!

1. Preheat the oven to 350°F. Line a baking sheet with parchment paper.

2. Prepare the Vanilla Almond Sugar Cookie dough.

3. On a lightly floured surface, roll out the dough ¼ inch thick.

4. Cut out cookies using the rocket ship cookie cutter (A). (If you don't have a rocket ship cookie cutter, use the template on page 252 or the QR code to make a stencil.) Save the excess dough.

5. Place the cookies on the lined baking sheet and push the lollipop sticks lightly into the dough (B).

6. Place a small piece of the excess dough on the back of the cookies to secure the lollipop sticks (C).

7. Bake the cookies until firm to the touch but not browned at the edges, 7 to 9 minutes.

8. Let the cookies cool on the baking sheet for 2 minutes, then transfer to a wire rack to cool completely.

SCAN
for Rocket
Ship Cookie
Template

TIME TO DECORATE!

1. Make the Royal Icing. Divide the icing among 5 bowls. Tint each bowl with a different food coloring: red, yellow, sky blue, light gray, and dark gray. For the light and dark gray, add one drop of black food coloring at a time until you reach the desired shades.

2. Scoop the icings into separate decorating bags fitted with #1 tips.

3. Pipe the red icing onto the fins and the nose cone (D).

4. Pipe the light gray icing onto the body of the rocket ship. You can use a toothpick to help spread it evenly (E).

5. Let the cookies sit at room temperature until the icing is completely hardened, about 1 hour.

6. Pipe a dark gray base onto the bottom of each rocket ship. Pipe yellow flames under the base. Pipe small dots of the light gray icing to look like metal rivets. Pipe a solid circle with the blue icing to look like a window (F), then outline it with dark gray.

7. Let the cookies set for 1 hour before serving.

GALAXY
CUPCAKES

·

PICTURES OF OUR GALAXY SHOW BEAUTIFUL swirls of deep blacks and vibrant purples, in many cases captured by spacecraft like the Hubble Space Telescope. As light enters Hubble's sensors, images are layered over one another and color is added to give our corner of the universe a breathtaking hue filled with stars and colliding supernovas. Take a little bit of that magic and top your favorite cupcake recipe for a truly out-of-this-world experience!

THE THINGS YOU'LL NEED

Rich Chocolate Cake batter (page 27)

3 tubs (16 ounces each) buttercream frosting

Food coloring gels: electric pink, electric purple, regal purple, royal blue, and black

Light blue sanding sugar

Edible silver stars (Wilton)

Muffin tin(s)

Black cupcake liners

6 decorating bags

#4B decorating tip

TO HELP THE FROSTING HOLD ITS SHAPE *better, try stirring in a little bit of powdered sugar.*

LET'S GET STARTED!

1. Preheat the oven to 350°F. Line 24 cups of 2 muffin tins with black paper liners. (Or line 12 cups of 1 muffin tin and bake in two batches.)

2. Prepare the Rich Chocolate Cake batter.

3. Fill each muffin cup two-thirds full with batter **A**.

4. Bake until a wooden pick inserted in the center of a cupcake comes out clean, 18 to 20 minutes.

5. Let the cupcakes cool completely before decorating.

TIME TO DECORATE!

1. Divide the buttercream frosting among 5 bowls. Tint each bowl with a different food coloring: electric pink, electric purple, regal purple, royal blue, and black **B**.

2. Scoop the frostings into 5 different decorating bags with no tips. Then pipe strips of the frostings into a single decorating bag fitted with a #4B tip. Be careful to keep the frosting colors separate **C**.

3. Frost the cupcakes by starting on the outside and spiraling your way toward the center **D**. When you reach the middle, release the pressure and let the frosting taper off.

4. Sprinkle the light blue sanding sugar over the frosting **E**.

5. Sprinkle the edible silver stars on top **F**.

CHAPTER THREE

FANTASY

· & ·

SCI-FI

UNICORN POOP
COOKIES

UH-OH, LOOKS LIKE SOMEONE LEFT YOU A PRESENT. But what kind of animal poops rainbows? There's only one that I know of—the majestic unicorn! This cream cheese cookie dough was developed to be soft enough to mold, but firm enough to hold a poop shape while baking. My little sister, Molly, loves unicorns, and when asked in kindergarten what she wanted to be when she grew up, she proudly responded, "A unicorn trainer." To this very day, she still does.

THE THINGS YOU'LL NEED

Cream Cheese Sugar Cookie dough (page 33)

Food coloring gels: electric yellow, electric orange, electric pink, electric green, sky blue, and purple

White sugar pearls

Rainbow daisy sprinkles (Wilton)

Nonstick baking sheet

KEEP THE DOUGH CHILLING *in the refrigerator as often as possible during each step. This dough is sticky.*

1. Make the Cream Cheese Sugar Cookie dough.

2. Divide the dough into 6 even portions. Tint each portion with a different food coloring: electric yellow, electric orange, electric pink, electric green, sky blue, and purple **A**.

3. Wrap each colored dough tightly in plastic wrap and refrigerate for 1 hour.

4. Roll each colored dough into a log on top of a piece of wax paper.

5. Cut each dough log into 12 equal sections and roll each section into a ball **B**. Place the balls in the refrigerator for 15 minutes.

6. Gently roll the balls into 5-inch logs on wax paper **C**.

7. Stack the colored logs three across and two high: yellow, orange, and pink on the bottom; green, blue, and purple on the top **D**. Refrigerate for 20 minutes.

8. Preheat the oven to 350°F.

9. Gently twist and roll the colored dough until smooth **E**.

10. Curl each log into a spiral poop shape, placing the end over the top **F**. Transfer the cookies to a nonstick baking sheet and refrigerate for 10 minutes. Then freeze for 2 minutes to help the cookies hold their shape while baking.

11. Bake until the cookies are set and dry but not browned, about 11 minutes.

12. Let the cookies cool on the baking sheet for 2 minutes, then transfer to a wire rack to cool slightly (you want to decorate while they are still warm).

~~~~~~~ **TIME TO DECORATE!** ~~~~~~~

1. Place the white sugar pearls on the cookies while they are still warm.

2. Sprinkle the rainbow daisy sprinkles on top of the cookies, then let them cool completely.

CASTLE CAKE

I'VE ALWAYS ENJOYED MEDIEVAL stories, whether in books, films, or television shows. I got to explore castles up close and personal on a trip to Ireland, where many are over 800 years old. Cake might not last 800 years, but you can still build the perfect medieval fortress cake to defend the land from frosting dragons. They're very dangerous, you know.

THE THINGS YOU'LL NEED

Butter and flour, for the pan

2 batches Pound Cake batter (page 24)

7 tubs (16 ounces each) buttercream frosting

16 cereal treats (Rice Krispies Treats; 0.78 ounce each)

2 batches Marshmallow Fondant (page 37)

Food coloring gels: black, brown, leaf green, and pink

Powdered sugar, for dusting

5 ice cream sugar cones (Keebler)

6 x 6-inch metal baking pan

Muffin tin

1 cupcake liner

Cake leveler

2-inch round cookie cutter

⅞ x ½-inch rectangle cookie cutter

Wood-texture mold (Wilton)

2 decorating bags

#3 decorating tip

#13 decorating tip

#65 decorating tip (optional)

RO TIP

FONDANT DRIES OUT QUICKLY. WHEN NOT USING *it, wrap it tightly in plastic wrap or place it in an airtight container or bag.*

1. Preheat the oven to 325°F. Grease a 6 x 6-inch metal baking pan. Line the bottom with parchment paper, grease the paper, and flour the pan.

2. Make two batches of the Pound Cake batter.

3. Pour one-fifth of the batter into the baking pan and bake until a wooden pick inserted in the center of a cake comes out clean, about 50 minutes.

4. Cool the cake in the pan on a wire rack for 15 minutes. If necessary, loosen the cake from the sides of the pan with a small knife. Carefully flip the cake upside down onto the wire rack, peel off the parchment paper, and then turn the cake right side up onto the rack to cool completely. Repeat until you have 5 cakes.

5. Line 1 cup of a muffin tin with a paper liner and fill it two-thirds full with batter. Bake until a wooden pick inserted in the center of a cake comes out clean, about 16 minutes. Cool on a wire rack.

6. Once the square cakes have cooled, level off the tops with a cake leveler or large knife to create 1-inch-high layers.

7. Stack 3 of the 6-inch square cakes with a thin layer of buttercream frosting in between the layers **(A)**.

8. Trim the remaining 2 square cakes to make two 4-inch squares.

9. Stack the two 4-inch square cakes on top of the 6-inch layers, centered, with a thin layer of frosting between the layers **(B)**.

10. Remove the liner from the cupcake. Trim the cupcake with the round cookie cutter or a sharp knife to make a straight-sided cylinder about 2 inches in diameter.

11. Frost the top of the cake and center the cupcake cylinder on top **(C)**.

12. Frost the entire cake with a thin layer of frosting **(D)**.

13. Make 4 towers: For each tower, press 4 Rice Krispies Treats together and roll them into a cylinder **(E)**.

14. Place the Rice Krispies towers onto each corner of the cake, and frost with a thin layer of frosting **(F)**.

1. Prepare two batches of the Marshmallow Fondant. Mix three-quarters of the fondant with black food coloring, one drop at a time, until you reach the desired shade of gray. Mix a tablespoon of fondant with black food coloring to get pure black. Mix the remaining fondant with brown food coloring to get a brown "wood" color. Tightly wrap the black and brown fondant in plastic wrap and set aside.

2. Sprinkle powdered sugar onto wax paper. Roll out the gray fondant ⅛ inch thick and cut it into small rectangles, ⅞ x ½ inch each (G). You can use a cookie cutter or a sharp knife. I made 655 rectangles: 620 to cover my castle, and 35 for more decoration (step 8). Tightly wrap the remaining gray fondant with plastic wrap and set it aside for step 4.

3. Place the gray fondant rectangles onto the cake to look like stone bricks (H). If the frosting is dry, apply a little water to the back of the fondant rectangles to help them stick to the castle walls. Save the remaining rectangles for step 8.

4. Roll out the reserved gray fondant to ¼ inch thick and cut out the same size rectangles, ⅞ x ½ inch. Place these on top of the cake walls as battlements. (I use 26 rectangles to make my battlements.)

5. Sprinkle powdered sugar onto wax paper. Roll out the brown fondant into a ⅛-inch-thick round and press it into the wood-texture mold. Cut out a door and 3 windows with a sharp knife. Use a small amount of the black fondant to make the door details (I).

6. Place the door and windows on the front of the castle.

7. Invert the sugar cones on the top of the 4 towers and on the very top of the castle (J). Press the cones lightly into the frosting to secure them.

8. Cut the reserved bricks (from step 3) in half to create squares. Place the squares around the base of the cones to cover any frosting (K). (I use 35 rectangles to get 70 square bricks.)

9. Tint three-quarters of a tub of buttercream frosting with leaf green food coloring until you reach the desired shade of green.

10. Scoop the green frosting into a decorating bag fitted with a #3 tip and pipe on vines around the castle (L). Optional: Use a #65 tip to pipe on leaves with the green frosting.

11. Tint the remaining one-quarter tub of buttercream frosting with pink food coloring until you reach the desired shade of pink.

12. Scoop the pink frosting into a decorating bag fitted with a #13 tip and pipe flowers onto the vines.

CAULDRON
CAKE POPS

BOIL, BUBBLE, TOIL, AND TROUBLE—it's a magic cauldron cake pop for all your wizarding needs! In fantasy tales, cauldrons are used to brew potions and conjure enchantments, but historically they were used for cooking and boiling regular, nonmagical food. They are also featured prominently during Halloween, my number one favorite holiday. Your cauldron can be filled with just about anything—magic, gold, candy, who knows!

THE THINGS YOU'LL NEED

Rich Chocolate Cake batter (page 27)

6 ounces cream cheese, at room temperature, or 1 tub (16 ounces) buttercream frosting

1 bag (12 ounces) black Candy Melts (Wilton)

Royal Icing (page 36)

Food coloring gels: leaf green, red, orange, and black

Small crunchy candies (Nerds): green

9 x 13-inch metal baking pan

Baking sheet

Lollipop sticks

4 decorating bags

Three #2 decorating tips

#1 decorating tip

Foam block

YOU CAN MAKE THE CONTENTS OF THE *cauldron any color you want!*

LET'S GET STARTED!

1. Bake the Rich Chocolate Cake batter in a 9 x 13-inch metal baking pan as directed. Let the cake cool in the pan.

2. In a bowl, crumble the cake with your fingers.

3. Add the cream cheese or frosting to the crumbled cake and mix until evenly combined. (Use cream cheese if you like your cake balls more tart or use the frosting if you like them sweeter.)

4. Line a baking sheet with wax paper. Roll the cake mixture into balls (about 1½ inches) and place on the lined baking sheet.

5. Freeze the cake balls until set, about 30 minutes.

6. In the microwave or a double boiler, melt a small amount (about 5 ounces) of the black Candy Melts. Dip the ends of the lollipop sticks in the melted candy (it acts as an adhesive) and push the sticks halfway into the cake balls.

7. Place the cake pops in the refrigerator for about 30 minutes to chill.

TIME TO DECORATE!

1. Melt the remainder of the black Candy Melts. Dip the cake pops into the melted candy to cover them in black, letting the excess candy drip back into the bowl **A**.

2. Immediately place the cake pops on the lined baking sheet **B**. This will create a flat surface on the top of your cake pop, which will be the rim of the cauldron.

3. Make the Royal Icing. Divide the icing among 4 bowls. Tint each bowl with leaf green, red, orange, and black. Scoop the red, green, and black icings into separate decorating bags fitted with #2 tips. Scoop the orange icing into a decorating bag fitted with a #1 tip.

4. Pipe the red icing onto the bottom of each cauldron to look like flames. Pipe the orange icing on top of the red icing for more detail **C**.

5. Flip the pops upright and stick the lollipop sticks into a foam block to secure them. Pipe 2 small circles with the black icing on opposite sides of each cauldron to create the handles **D**.

6. Pipe the green icing on top of the cake pops **E**.

7. Place green Nerds on top to look like bubbles **F**. I use baking tweezers for more placement control.

TREASURE CHEST
CAKE

·

AT THE END OF A DUNGEON or a difficult quest? Or maybe you're digging up some buried treasure? Either way, chances are you'll find your prize locked away in a treasure chest! Treasure chests are a mainstay of video games and fantasy worlds, where loot of all kinds is hidden for brave adventurers to find. So whether you're saving the kingdom or sailing the seven seas, remember this handy chocolate chest cake—for all your loot stashing needs.

THE THINGS YOU'LL NEED

Butter and flour, for the pan

4 batches Rich Chocolate Cake batter (page 27)

3 tubs (16 ounces each) chocolate frosting

24 cereal treats (Rice Krispies Treats; 0.78 ounce each)

2 batches Marshmallow Fondant (page 37)

Brown food coloring gel

Powdered sugar, for dusting

1 box (about 14 ounces) graham crackers (Honey Maid)

1 tub (16 ounces) vanilla frosting

Chocolate coins and Ring Pops

9 x 13-inch metal baking pan

Cake leveler

Cake tray

Cardboard

6-inch cookie sticks

1. Preheat the oven to 325°F. Grease a 9 x 13-inch metal baking pan. Line the bottom with parchment paper, grease the paper, and flour the pan.

2. Make the Rich Chocolate Cake batter.

3. Pour half of the batter into the baking pan and bake until a wooden pick inserted in the center of the cake comes out clean, about 50 minutes.

4. Cool in the pan on a wire rack for 15 minutes. If necessary, loosen the cake from the sides of the pan with a small knife. Carefully flip the cake upside down onto the wire rack, peel off the parchment paper, and then turn the cake right side up onto the rack to cool completely.

5. Repeat to make a second cake.

6. Once both cakes have cooled, level off the tops with a cake leveler or large knife (A).

7. Cut the cakes in half crosswise to make a total of four 6½ x 9-inch cakes (B).

8. From one of the cake layers, cut out a rectangle about 3 x 7½ inches, with a ¾-inch border on three sides (C). This creates a space to stash the loot.

9. Stack the remaining 3 cakes with a thin layer of chocolate frosting between the layers. Place the cut-out layer on top, with the thicker portion toward the back of the treasure chest (D).

10. Mold the Rice Krispies Treats together into a rounded treasure chest lid that matches the dimensions of the cakes, about 6½ x 9 inches. Cut a piece of cardboard to match the dimensions of the lid and place the lid on the cardboard (E).

11. Frost the entire cake and the lid with a thin layer of chocolate frosting (F).

1. Prepare two batches of the Marshmallow Fondant. Tint three-quarters of the fondant with brown food coloring until you reach the desired shade of dark brown. Tint the remaining fondant light brown. Tightly wrap the light brown fondant in plastic wrap and set it aside. (Optional: Before tinting the fondant, set aside a small amount to make a pearl necklace; see step 10.)

2. Sprinkle powdered sugar onto wax paper. Roll out the dark brown fondant ⅛ inch thick and cut it into 1½-inch-wide strips with a sharp knife (G).

3. Wrap the strips around the cake and lid to look like wooden boards (H). If the frosting is already dry, apply a little water to the back of the fondant to make the strips stick.

4. Insert 2 cookie sticks several inches apart toward the front edge of the cut-out portion of the cake. Carefully place the lid on top so it is slightly open (I).

5. Sprinkle powdered sugar onto wax paper. Roll out the light brown fondant ⅛ inch thick and cut it into ⅞-inch-wide strips with a sharp knife. Roll the scraps of light brown fondant into ¼-inch balls.

6. Optional: Make a lock out of light brown fondant for the front of the chest.

7. Place the light brown fondant strips onto the chest to look like brass bindings. Place the small fondant balls on the strips to look like rivets (J).

8. Using a blender or your hands, grind the graham crackers to a fine dust.

9. Place the treasure chest on a cake tray. Frost the cake tray with the vanilla frosting. Sprinkle on graham cracker crumbs to look like sand (K).

10. Place assorted candies into the chest. I use Ring Pops, white fondant rolled into balls to look like a pearl necklace, and chocolate coins (L).

RO TIP

USE WHATEVER ASSORTED CANDIES YOU LIKE *for the loot in the treasure chest.*

LOCH NESS
CUPCAKES

WHAT'S THAT OUT THERE IN THE LAKE? Is it a really big fish, a late-night swimmer . . . or something else? Many have opted for "something else," and that something is Nessie, the Loch Ness Monster. Nessie is what scientists call a cryptid—a suggested animal that hasn't been discovered yet, like the Sasquatch or the Chupacabra. Some say she's real and some say she's not, but either way, this local legend is renowned the world over. Maybe you can coax her out with a cupcake—who knows, she might just have a sweet tooth!

THE THINGS YOU'LL NEED

White Cake batter (page 25)

2 tubs (16 ounces each) buttercream frosting

Food color gels: royal blue, sky blue, and black

Blue sanding sugar

Marshmallow Fondant (page 37)

Shortening, for greasing your hands

Muffin tin(s)

Black cupcake liners

3 decorating bags

#6B decorating tip

Toothpicks

RO·TIP

THE MORE YOU HANDLE FONDANT, *the softer it gets. If it becomes too soft while molding, let it sit for 10 minutes.*

LET'S GET STARTED!

1. Preheat the oven to 350°F. Line 24 cups of 2 muffin tins with black paper liners. (Or use 1 muffin tin and bake in two batches.)

2. Prepare the White Cake batter.

3. Fill each muffin cup two-thirds full with batter.

4. Bake until a wooden pick inserted in the center of a cupcake comes out clean, 18 to 20 minutes.

5. Let the cupcakes cool completely before decorating.

TIME TO DECORATE!

1. Divide the buttercream frosting between 2 bowls. Use the food coloring to tint one bowl a dark blue and the other bowl a light blue (A).

2. Scoop each frosting into a decorating bag with no tip. Take those bags and use them to pipe both blue frostings, side by side, into a third decorating bag fitted with a #6B tip (B).

3. Frost the cupcakes by starting on the outside and spiraling your way toward the center. When you reach the middle, release the pressure and let the frosting taper off. Use a spatula to smooth the frosting to look like waves (C).

4. Sprinkle the blue sanding sugar onto the frosting (D).

5. Prepare the Marshmallow Fondant. Coat your hands with shortening so the food coloring doesn't stain them, then tint the fondant gray by kneading in one drop of black food coloring at a time until you reach the desired shade.

6. Mold the gray fondant into the form of the Loch Ness Monster (the parts that would show above the water) and stick toothpicks in the bottom of each piece. Stick the dorsal spikes onto Nessie's back by wetting the fondant with a little water (E).

7. Insert the toothpicks into the cupcakes (F).

8. Arrange the cupcakes into the shape of Loch Ness, with Nessie swimming through the middle of it.

ROBOT
BROWNIE POPS

·

CAN A ROBOT LEARN TO BAKE? Probably! Robotics is a huge field of science and technology, with new models being created every year. My nickname is Robot, though it's not because I'm a Cylon (I swear). R2-D2 from *Star Wars*, Data from *Star Trek*, and Bumblebee from *Transformers* are among some of my favorite fictional robots. This dessert will really get your gears turning!

THE THINGS YOU'LL NEED

Butter, for greasing the pan

2 batches Brownie batter (page 30)

1 bag (12 ounces) white Candy Melts (Wilton)

1 bag (12 ounces) black Candy Melts (Wilton)

Red licorice laces

2 packages candy eyeballs (Wilton)

Black jelly beans (Jelly Belly)

Black licorice pastilles

Small candy-coated chocolates (M&M's Minis): red, blue, and green

Gummy rings (Life Savers Gummies): red, green, and orange

9 x 13-inch metal baking pan

70 lollipop sticks

Foam block

1. Preheat the oven to 350°F. Grease a 9 x 13-inch metal baking pan and line it with parchment paper.

2. Prepare two batches of the Brownie batter. Pour the batter into the prepared pan and spread evenly.

3. Bake until a wooden pick inserted in the center comes out mostly clean, 38 to 40 minutes.

4. Let the brownies cool in the pan.

5. Remove the brownies from the pan, peel off the parchment paper, and cut the brownies into 1¼ x 1¼-inch cubes. Pack the cubes gently with your hands to make them firmer and more condensed Ⓐ.

~~~~~~~~~~ **TIME TO DECORATE!** ~~~~~~~~~~

1. In the microwave or a double boiler, melt the white and black Candy Melts together to make a light gray color (I use a ratio of 9 white to 1 black).

2. Dip an end of each lollipop stick into the gray melts (it acts as an adhesive), then insert it halfway into a brownie cube Ⓑ. Place brownie pops in the refrigerator for about 30 minutes to chill.

3. Dip the brownie pops into the gray melts, making sure to cover them completely Ⓒ. Stand the dipped squares in a foam block to dry.

4. Cut the red licorice laces into ½-inch lengths. Using a dab of gray candy as an adhesive, attach the licorice to the pops as mouths.

5. Adhere the candy eyeballs to the pops with a dab of gray candy Ⓓ.

6. Cut the jelly beans in half crosswise and use a dab of gray candy to stick the halves to the sides of the brownie pops for ears.

7. Press a black licorice pastille into the top center of each pop. Attach one M&M's Mini on top of the pastille as the antenna Ⓔ. I use red, green, and blue M&M's.

8. Place the Life Savers Gummies onto the bottom of the pops as necks, using a dab of gray candy Ⓕ. I use red, green, and orange gummies.

UFO CAKE POPS

UNIDENTIFIED FLYING OBJECTS (UFOS) have fascinated people for generations. A wide range of UFOs appear in many of my favorite science-fiction movies: *Independence Day*, *War of the Worlds*, *District 9*, and countless others! You can use any candy you want to decorate your UFO Cake Pops for the impending taste invasion. The only thing identifiable about these pops is that they're delicious!

THE THINGS YOU'LL NEED

White Cake batter (page 25)

6 ounces cream cheese, or 1 tub (16 ounces) buttercream frosting

1 bag (12 ounces) black Candy Melts (Wilton)

1 bag (12 ounces) white Candy Melts (Wilton)

Black licorice gumdrops

Small candy-coated chocolates (M&M's Minis): red, blue, green, orange, and yellow

9 x 13-inch metal baking pan

Baking sheet

Lollipop sticks

Foam block

RO TIP

IF YOUR DIPPED POPS DRY BEFORE YOU ADD *the black licorice gumdrop, use a dab of Candy Melts on the bottom of the gumdrop to act as an adhesive.*

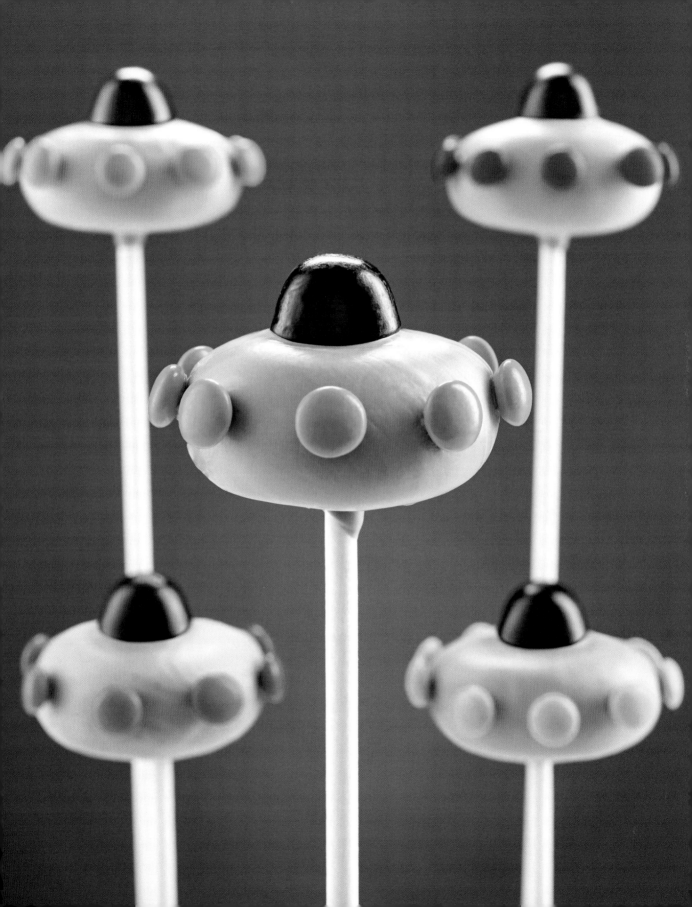

LET'S GET STARTED!

1. Bake the White Cake batter in a 9 x 13-inch metal baking pan as directed. Let the cake cool completely in the pan.

2. In a bowl, crumble the cake with your fingers.

3. Add the cream cheese or frosting and mix until evenly combined. (Use cream cheese if you like your cake pops more tart or use the frosting if you like them sweeter.)

4. Line a baking sheet with wax paper. Roll the mixture into balls (about 1½ inches in diameter) and place them on the lined baking sheet (A).

5. Flatten the balls into thick disks (B).

6. Refrigerate the cake disks for 30 minutes to set.

TIME TO DECORATE!

1. In the microwave or a double boiler, melt the white and black Candy Melts together to make a light gray color (I use a ratio of 4 white to 1 black).

2. Dip the end of the lollipop sticks into the gray melts to help act as an adhesive and press the sticks halfway into the cake disks (C).

3. Dip the cake pops into the gray melts, making sure to cover completely. Let the excess candy drip back into the bowl (D). Stand the dipped pops in a foam block to dry.

4. While the candy melt coating on the pop is still wet, place a black licorice gumdrop on the top of each pop (E).

5. Dab a small amount of gray candy onto the back of the M&M's and carefully place around the sides of the cake pops as lights (F).

ZOMBIE BRAIN CAKE

WALKERS, THE UNDEAD, OR WHATEVER you prefer to call them, there's nothing like a zombie to liven the party. Or . . . deaden the party. You may know them from video games, television, or movies, where these scary shamblers result from genetic experiments and secret projects gone wrong. At least one thing is for sure: Zombies love brains. So bite back and show them who's boss with this zombie brain cake!

THE THINGS YOU'LL NEED

Butter, for greasing the bowl

Red Velvet Cake batter (page 26)

1 tub (16 ounces) cream cheese frosting

Marshmallow Fondant (page 37)

1 cup light corn syrup

1½ teaspoons unsweetened cocoa powder

Red food coloring gel

1½-quart ovenproof glass bowl (Pyrex)

Cake tester

RO TIP AN ALTERNATIVE TO THE FAKE BLOOD *recipe is seedless raspberry jam.*

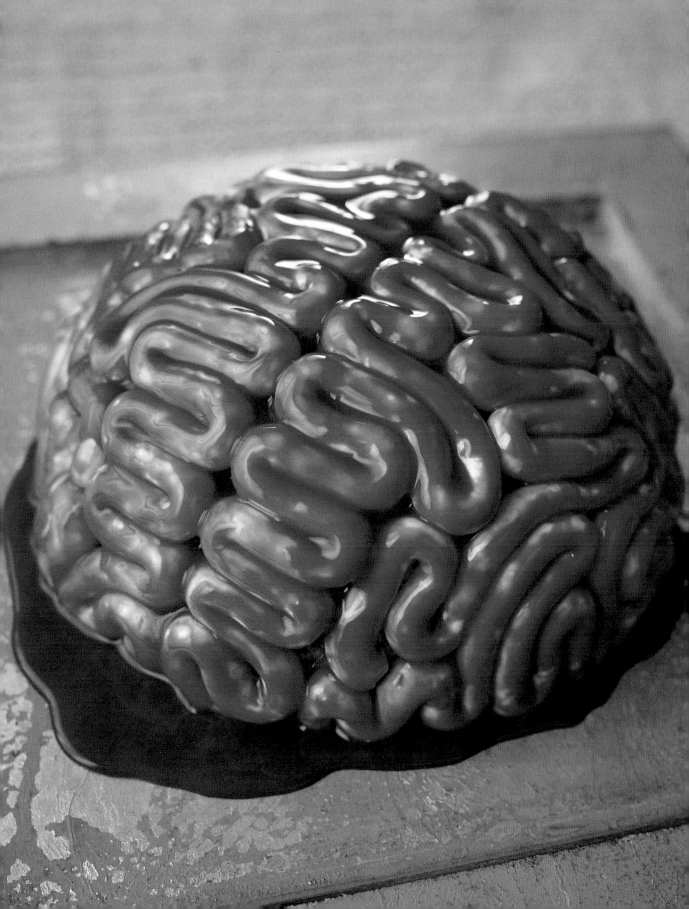

LET'S GET STARTED!

1. Preheat the oven to 300°F. Grease a 1½-quart ovenproof glass bowl.

2. Prepare the Red Velvet Cake batter.

3. Pour the batter into the greased glass bowl until it is two-thirds full. You will have a little leftover batter.

4. Slow-bake until a cake tester inserted in the center comes out clean, about 1 hour 30 minutes.

5. Let the cake cool and then remove it from the bowl. Level the top with a large knife (A) and place the cake, flat side down, on a cake plate.

6. Frost the cake with a very thin layer of cream cheese frosting (B).

TIME TO DECORATE!

1. Prepare the Marshmallow Fondant (C).

2. Roll out the fondant into ½-inch-thick ropes and arrange them on the cake to look like a brain (D).

3. Make fake blood by mixing the corn syrup, cocoa powder, and red food coloring (E).

4. Brush the fake blood over the fondant with a paintbrush (F).

CHAPTER FOUR

GAMING

· GAMING ·

VIDEO GAME
CONTROLLER
COOKIES

·

LOOKING FOR AN EDIBLE GIFT IDEA for the gamer in your life? These controller cookies will do the trick—you can make them look like any kind of controller with icing and candy buttons. You can also model them after your favorite gaming system's controller, or you can design your own. This treat will take it to the next level!

THE THINGS YOU'LL NEED

Vanilla Almond Sugar Cookie dough
   (page 34)

Royal Icing (page 36)

Black food coloring gel

Candy-coated chocolates (M&M's)

Small candy-coated chocolates
   (M&M's Minis)

Baking sheet

4½ x 3-inch rectangle cookie cutter

3 decorating bags

Three #2 decorating tips

RO TIP YOU CAN USE ANY ROUND CANDIES *you'd like for the buttons.*

LET'S GET STARTED!

1. Preheat the oven to 350°F. Line a baking sheet with parchment paper.

2. Prepare the Vanilla Almond Sugar Cookie dough.

3. On a lightly floured surface, roll out the dough ¼ inch thick.

4. Cut out cookies using the rectangle cookie cutter (A).

5. To turn some of these rectangles into smaller controllers trim off a 1-inch strip from one long side of the cookie (B). Gather those scraps and re-roll to cut out more controllers.

6. Place the cookies on the lined baking sheet and bake until firm to the touch but not browned at the edges, 7 to 9 minutes.

7. Let the cookies cool on the baking sheet for 2 minutes, then transfer to a wire rack to cool completely.

TIME TO DECORATE!

1. Make the Royal Icing and divide it among 3 bowls. Mix in black food coloring, one drop at a time, to make light gray, dark gray, and black icings.

2. Scoop the icings into separate decorating bags fitted with #2 tips.

3. Outline the cookies with the black icing (C).

4. Once the outline has hardened, fill in the cookie centers with the black icing (D). You can use a toothpick to help spread it evenly.

5. Let the cookies sit at room temperature until the icing is completely hardened, about 1 hour.

6. On the larger cookies, pipe on a dark gray square for the LCD screen. Pipe on a light gray D-pad and buttons. On the smaller cookies, pipe on a light gray D-pad (E).

7. Pipe a dab of black icing on the back of the M&M's and place them on your cookies as the buttons. Use the M&M's Minis for the larger cookies and the regular-size M&M's for the smaller cookies (F).

MANA & HEALTH
POTIONS

IT'S IMPORTANT FOR THE RAMPAGING BARBARIAN or immortal sorcerer in your life to properly hydrate, which is where health and mana potions come in. I've always loved playing adventure games and dungeon crawlers, and these Italian cream sodas really hit the spot when you're tanking a boss or running out of spell juice. Remember: red for hit points, blue for magic. One mix-up and you might find yourself on the business end of a total party wipe.

THE THINGS YOU'LL NEED

Blue raspberry syrup (Torani)

Red raspberry syrup (Torani)

Club soda

Half-and-half

Black felt-tip pen

White or beige stick-on labels

Lighter or candle

Glass bottles

RO TIP YOU CAN USE DIFFERENT FLAVORED SYRUPS *to make different kinds of potions.*

1. With a black marker, write "Mana" on half of your stick-on labels and "Health" on the other half in a script-style font (A).

2. Lightly burn the edges of the labels with a candle or lighter for an antiqued look (B).

3. Place the labels onto the middle of the bottles (C).

4. Fill each "Mana" bottle one-third full with blue raspberry syrup (D). Fill each "Health" bottle one-third full with red raspberry syrup.

5. Fill the bottles with club soda, leaving a little room at the top (E).

6. Top off each bottle with a splash of half-and-half (F).

CHOCOLATE
CHESS CAKE

My friend **KURT**

WHEN I DECIDED TO MAKE a chess cake on my show, I knew I had to make it playable—so I invited my friend Kurt Hugo Schneider to help me do it. Kurt is best known as a music producer, but he was also a U.S. national chess master at the age of 15. We made this cake together and played a few games. He beat me blindfolded every time and ate all my pieces. Cake-mate!

THE THINGS YOU'LL NEED

Butter, for greasing the pan

2 batches Rich Chocolate Cake batter (page 27)

3 pounds white chocolate chips

3 pounds dark chocolate chips

4 tubs (16 ounces each) chocolate frosting

12 x 12-inch baking pan

Cake leveler

2 plastic squeeze bottles

1½-inch square candy mold (CybrTrayd)

3-D chess pieces chocolate mold (CybrTrayd)

Decorating comb #1446

2 decorating bags

#4B decorating tip

#22 decorating tip

RO·TIP

REMEMBER, WHEN PLAYING *a game of chess, white chocolate always goes first.*

LET'S GET STARTED!

1. Preheat the oven to 325°F. Grease a 12 x 12-inch baking pan and line the bottom with parchment paper.

2. Make the Rich Chocolate Cake batter.

3. Pour the batter into the baking pan and bake for 30 minutes. Reduce the oven temperature to 300°F and bake until a wooden pick inserted in the center of the cake comes out clean, about 1 hour 15 minutes longer.

4. Cool in the pan on a wire rack for 15 minutes. If necessary, loosen the cake from the sides of the pan with a small knife. Carefully invert the cake out of the pan onto the rack, peel off the paper, and turn it right side up onto the rack to cool completely.

5. Level off the top with a cake leveler or large knife.

TIME TO DECORATE!

1. In the microwave or a double boiler, melt the white and dark chocolates separately, and pour each into a plastic squeeze bottle.

2. Using the bottles, fill the square candy molds with chocolate Ⓐ. Use a toothpick to wiggle the chocolate evenly. Tap the tray on the work surface to get rid of any air bubbles. Place in the refrigerator for 45 minutes to 1 hour to set.

3. Pop the squares out of the molds. Repeat until you have 32 of both colors.

4. Meanwhile, fill the chess set molds with white and dark chocolate. Use a toothpick to wiggle the chocolate evenly Ⓑ. Tap the tray on the work surface to get rid of any air bubbles. Place in the refrigerator for 45 minutes to 1 hour to set.

5. Pop the chess pieces out of the molds. Repeat until you have enough paired pieces (to make 3-D figures) for 8 pawns, 2 rooks, 2 knights, 2 bishops, 1 queen, and 1 king of both white and dark chocolate. Stick the matching chess pieces together with dabs of melted chocolate Ⓒ.

6. Frost the cake with 2 tubs of the chocolate frosting Ⓓ. Run the large edge of the decorating comb along the sides to create horizontal ridges.

7. Arrange the white and dark chocolate squares on the top of the cake like a chess board Ⓔ.

8. Scoop 1 tub of chocolate frosting into a decorating bag fitted with a #4B tip, and pipe a trim along the bottom of the cake. Scoop the remaining tub of frosting into a decorating bag fitted with a #22 tip, and pipe a trim around the top edges of the cake Ⓕ. Place your chocolate chess pieces on top of the cake.

20-SIDED DICE
COOKIES

My friend FELICIA

THIS IS A COOKIE I HAD A LOT OF FUN making on my show with help from my friend Felicia Day. We share a love for all kinds of tabletop games, and 20-sided dice are used in many of these games, especially pen and paper role-playing ones like Dungeons & Dragons. When I was growing up, my family used to have game night every Sunday, and like these cookies, you can bet everyone went for "the good dice" as fast as possible!

THE THINGS YOU'LL NEED

Vanilla Almond Sugar Cookie dough
    (page 34)
2 batches Royal Icing (page 36)
Red liquid food coloring

Baking sheet
3½-inch hexagon cookie cutter
    (template on page 252 or QR code
    on page 164)
2 decorating bags
Two #2 decorating tips
#1 decorating tip

RO·TIP

A #1 DECORATING TIP IS IDEAL FOR *fine details like the numbers.*

LET'S GET STARTED!

1. Preheat the oven to 350°F. Line a baking sheet with parchment paper.

2. Prepare the Vanilla Almond Sugar Cookie dough.

3. On a lightly floured surface, roll out the dough ¼ inch thick.

4. Cut out as many cookies as you can using the hexagon cookie cutter. (If you don't have a hexagon cookie cutter, use the template on page 252 or the QR code to make a stencil.)

5. Place the cookies on the lined baking sheet and bake until firm to the touch but not browned at the edges, 7 to 9 minutes.

6. Let the cookies cool on the baking sheet for 2 minutes, then transfer to a wire rack to cool completely.

TIME TO DECORATE!

1. Make the Royal Icing. Leave one batch white and tint the second with red food coloring until you reach the desired shade of bright red Ⓐ. Scoop the red icing into a decorating bag fitted with a #2 tip and outline the cookies a little in from the edge Ⓑ.

2. Once the outline has hardened, fill in the center of the cookies with red icing Ⓒ. You can use a toothpick to help spread it evenly.

3. Scoop the white icing into a decorating bag fitted with a #2 tip. With the white icing, outline the hexagon. Connect every other point on the hexagon to make a triangle Ⓓ.

4. Pipe the remaining lines to complete the 20-sided dice pattern Ⓔ.

5. Switch to a #1 tip on the white icing, and pipe on the dice numbers Ⓕ.

FANTASY
SWEET ROLLS

HEROES IN A DISTANT LAND will often find themselves slaying dragons and thwarting the plans of nefarious madmen, which can build some serious appetite! Luckily, they can always count on a tasty sweet roll to get them back on the road. This recipe puts a fantasy twist on a classic cinnamon roll. Now your favorite adventurer can really start the day off right.

THE THINGS YOU'LL NEED

Sweet Cinnamon Roll dough (page 29)

4 tablespoons salted butter, melted

⅔ cup packed light brown sugar

1 tablespoon ground cinnamon

2¼ cups powdered sugar

1 teaspoon vanilla extract

3 tablespoons whole milk

Two 6-cavity mini fluted pans (Wilton)

YOU CAN USE A DECORATING BAG *for more control when pouring the glaze.*

LET'S GET STARTED!

1. Prepare the Sweet Cinnamon Roll dough through step 5 (the first rise).

2. On a lightly floured surface, roll the risen dough into a 12 x 18-inch rectangle and brush with the melted butter.

3. In a small bowl, combine the brown sugar and cinnamon. Sprinkle the sugar mixture evenly over the dough Ⓐ.

4. Fold the dough into thirds Ⓑ.

5. Cut the folded dough crosswise into 1-inch-wide slices Ⓒ.

6. Grease the pans first and then carefully wrap the slices around the center tubes in the mini fluted pan cavities Ⓓ.

7. Cover the pans with plastic wrap and let the rolls rise for 30 minutes.

8. Preheat the oven to 350°F.

9. Bake until the rolls are golden brown, 18 to 20 minutes.

10. Let the rolls cool in the pan for 10 minutes, then transfer to a wire rack to cool completely.

TIME TO DECORATE!

1. Level the bottom of the rolls with a large knife Ⓔ.

2. In a small bowl, combine the powdered sugar and vanilla. Slowly whisk in the milk until the glaze has a good spreadable consistency.

3. Drizzle the glaze over the top of the rolls Ⓕ.

RUPEE
HARD CANDIES

COLLECTING GEMS IS A COMMON FEATURE in many video games. They come in many different colors and are worth different amounts, so when making these hard candies you can make them look however you want! I used red, green, and blue, but yours can be purple, orange, or even gold!

THE THINGS YOU'LL NEED

6 cups sugar

1½ cups water

2¼ cups light corn syrup

Food coloring gels: leaf green, red, and sky blue

Flavorings: pineapple, strawberry, and cotton candy

Candy thermometer

Heatproof glass measuring cup (Pyrex)

Silicone gem mold

RO TIP MAKE SURE TO USE HEAT-RESISTANT TOOLS *when working with hard candy.*

1. In a medium saucepan, combine 2 cups of the sugar, ½ cup of the water, ¾ cup of the corn syrup, and leaf green food coloring to tint the mixture deep green **A**.

2. Whisk together over medium heat until the sugar is dissolved **B**.

3. Place a candy thermometer in the pan and continue cooking until the candy mixture reaches 275°F **C**.

4. Remove the pan from the heat and immediately mix in ½ teaspoon pineapple flavoring **D**.

5. Quickly pour the mixture into a heatproof measuring cup and then carefully pour it into the silicone gem mold **E**.

6. Let the candies set until completely hardened, about 45 minutes, then pop the gems out of the mold **F**.

7. Repeat the process to make red and blue gems. I use red food coloring and ½ teaspoon strawberry flavoring for the red gems, and sky blue food coloring and ½ teaspoon cotton candy flavoring for the blue gems.

HP
CANDY BARS

EVERY ADVENTURER KNOWS THEY'RE ONE CRITICAL HIT away from a game over, so why not keep a little pick-me-up on hand just in case? Get hit by a wayward spell? Take an axe to the face? Fall down a hole that you totally didn't see? If you're feeling low on hit points, grab an HP candy bar and you'll be back to fighting those giant spiders in no time.

THE THINGS YOU'LL NEED

1 bag (23 ounces) milk chocolate chips

1 bag (11 ounces) caramel melts

2 tablespoons heavy cream

Sea salt

36 mini shortbread cookies (Lorna Doone)

Royal Icing (page 36)

Food coloring gels: black, red, orange, yellow, and green

12-bar (3 x 1 x 1 inch) silicone candy mold (Fat Daddio's)

Baking sheet

6 decorating bags

Plastic squeeze bottle

Five #2 decorating tips

RO TIP YOU CAN CUSTOMIZE YOUR CANDY *bar with any ingredients!*

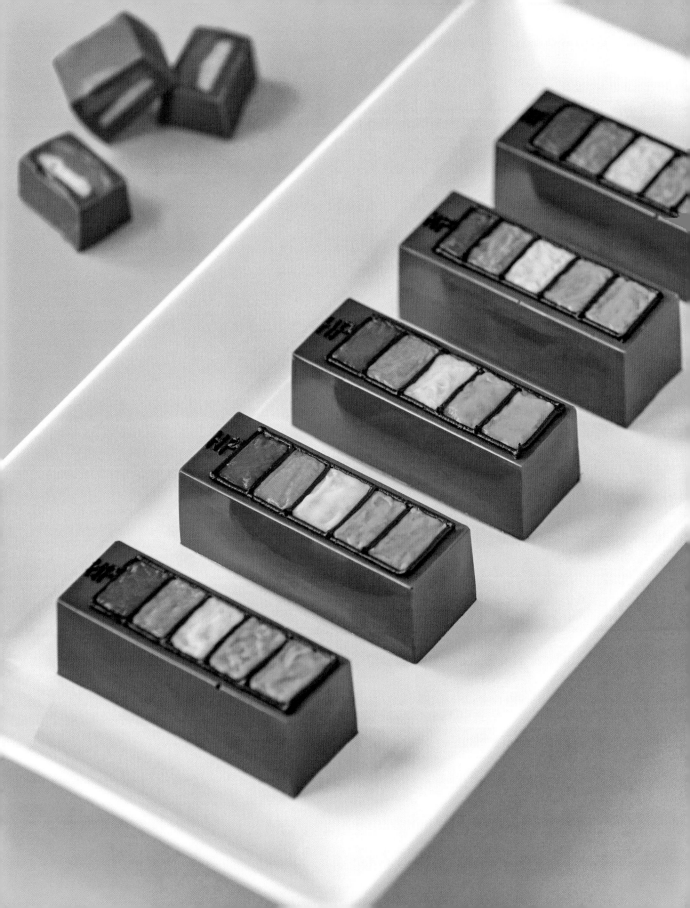

1. Place the silicone candy mold on a baking sheet.

2. In the microwave or a double boiler, melt the milk chocolate. Pour it into a decorating bag (with no tip).

3. Fill the rectangle molds one-quarter full with chocolate. Then, using a paintbrush, paint a layer of chocolate up the sides of each rectangle (A).

4. In a saucepan, combine the caramels and cream and melt over low heat, mixing thoroughly. Scoop the caramel mixture into a plastic squeeze bottle.

5. Using the plastic squeeze bottle, fill each mold to the halfway point with caramel (B). Sprinkle a pinch of sea salt over the caramel in each bar.

6. Place the shortbread cookies on top of the caramel for a crunchy layer (C).

7. Fill in the rest of the mold with milk chocolate (D). Gently tap the baking sheet on the counter to release any air bubbles.

8. Place the mold in the freezer for 10 minutes to set.

9. Pop the bars out of the silicone mold (E).

TIME TO DECORATE!

1. Make the Royal Icing and divide it among 5 bowls. Tint each bowl with a different food coloring: black, red, orange, yellow, and green. Scoop the icings into separate decorating bags fitted with #2 tips.

2. Use the black icing to outline the bars and to pipe "HP" on each one.

3. Fill in the HP levels with icing: 1 bar red, 1 bar orange, 1 bar yellow, and 2 bars green (F).

CAMOUFLAGE
FPS CUPCAKES

FIRST-PERSON SHOOTER (FPS) GAMES involve aiming and shooting at targets from the viewpoint of the main character. I played a ton of Wolfenstein 3D and Duke Nukem 3D growing up, and later GoldenEye 007 on Nintendo 64 with my sister. These days I'm taking down a lot of zombies in Left 4 Dead, so in honor of all the FPS games out there, I made these camo crosshair cupcakes. They'll really hit the spot!

THE THINGS YOU'LL NEED

1 bag (12 ounces) black Candy Melts (Wilton)

Small red candy-coated chocolates (M&M's Minis)

White Cake batter (page 25)

Food coloring gels: ivory, leaf green, black, and brown

2 tubs (16 ounces each) buttercream frosting

Crosshair template (page 252 or QR code on page 180)

Muffin tin(s)

Brown cupcake liners

1 regular decorating bag

5 large decorating bags

#2 decorating tip

#829 decorating tip

RO·TIP

YOU CAN USE ANY 4 COLORS *you like to make your own custom camouflage.*

1. Trace the crosshair template on page 252 onto a sheet of paper several times or print the template using the QR code. Place the template on a baking sheet and lay wax paper over the template Ⓐ.

2. In the microwave or a double boiler, melt the black Candy Melts. Scoop the melted candy into the regular decorating bag fitted with a #2 tip and trace the crosshair template. Place a red M&M's Mini in the center of each crosshair Ⓑ.

3. Place the crosshairs in the freezer for 20 minutes.

4. Preheat the oven to 350°F. Line 24 cups of 2 muffin tins with brown paper liners. (Or line 12 cups of 1 muffin tin and bake in two batches.)

5. Prepare the White Cake batter.

6. Divide the batter among 4 bowls. Tint each bowl with food coloring to make ivory, leaf green, black, and brown Ⓒ.

7. Scoop the 4 colored batters into separate large decorating bags and alternate adding the colored batters into the lined muffin cups, filling them two-thirds full Ⓓ.

8. Bake until a wooden pick inserted in the center of a cupcake comes out clean, 18 to 20 minutes.

9. Let the cupcakes cool completely before decorating.

SCAN
for Crosshair
Template

TIME TO DECORATE!

1. Divide the frosting among 4 bowls. Tint each bowl with the same 4 colors as the cake batter. Carefully scoop the frostings separately into a large decorating bag fitted with a #829 tip, trying not to let the frosting colors mix Ⓔ.

2. Frost the cupcakes. Start with the tip at an outer edge of the cupcake and move around the cupcake counterclockwise until you reach the middle, then release the pressure and let the frosting taper off Ⓕ.

3. Take the crosshairs out of the freezer when they are completely set and carefully insert them in the center of each cupcake.

TECH

· & ·

WEB

MOTHERBOARD
CAKE

A CHOCOLATE PROCESSOR OR CANDY MICROCHIPS won't make your computer work, but they can optimize your sweet tooth! Computers are a huge part of what makes our world run, but you don't have to be an engineer to make one yourself—many people build them on their own, creating the ultimate system for whatever their needs may be. Use your favorite candies to customize your motherboard cake to be the ultimate in edible hardware.

THE THINGS YOU'LL NEED

Butter, for greasing the pans

2 batches White Cake batter (page 25)

4 tubs (16 ounces each) buttercream frosting

Leaf green food coloring gel

Assorted candies (see list in step 1 of Time to Decorate)

Two 9 x 13-inch metal baking pans

Cake leveler

4 decorating bags

#4B decorating tip

#2 decorating tip

#3 decorating tip

#5 decorating tip

PRO TIP. MOTHERBOARDS COME IN ALL SHAPES *and sizes, so make your cake as big or small as you would like*

MOTHERBOARD CAKE BASICS

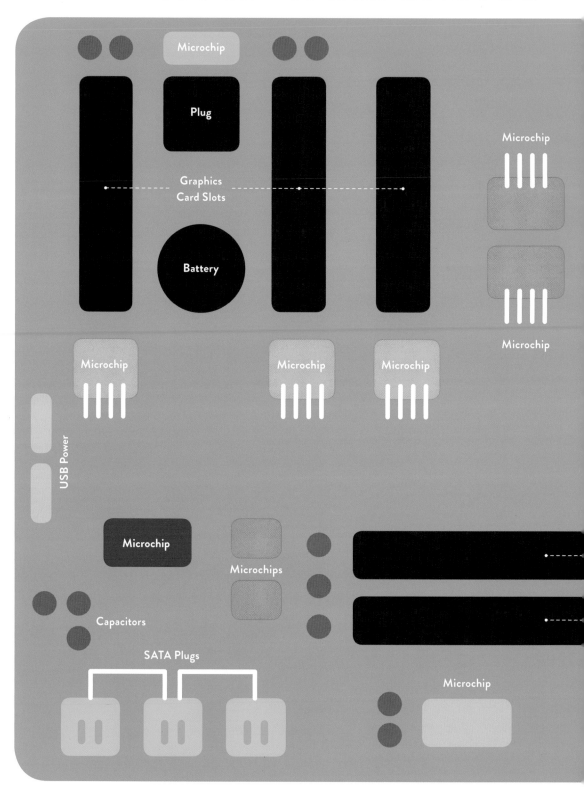

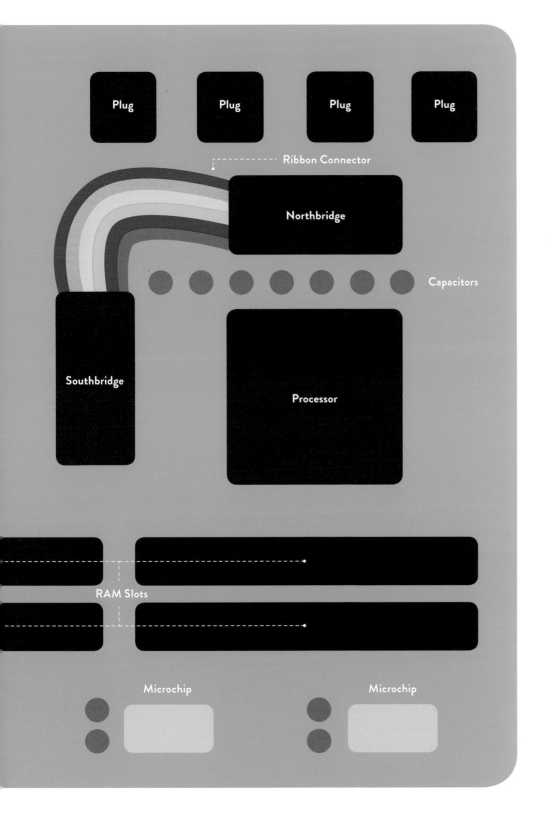

LET'S GET STARTED!

1. Preheat the oven to 350°F. Grease two 9 x 13-inch metal baking pans.

2. Make two batches of the White Cake batter and divide it evenly between the baking pans.

3. Bake until a wooden pick inserted in the center of a cake comes out clean, 30 to 35 minutes.

4. Let the cakes cool in the pans for 15 minutes. Run a small knife along the sides of the pan, then transfer the cakes to a wire rack to cool completely.

5. Level the tops of the cakes with a cake leveler or large knife Ⓐ.

6. Tint 3 tubs of the buttercream frosting with leaf green food coloring until you reach the desired shade of green. Scoop one-third of the green frosting into a decorating bag fitted with a #4B tip and set aside.

7. Place one cake on a platter or cake tray. Frost the top of the layer with green frosting and set the second cake on top of it Ⓑ.

8. Frost the top and sides of the entire cake with the green frosting Ⓒ.

9. Place the cake in the freezer for 20 to 30 minutes.

10. Remove the cake from the freezer and go over the frosting with a warm spatula to make a smooth surface for decorating.

TIME TO DECORATE!

1. Use your favorite candies to look like the pieces of a motherboard Ⓓ.

MICROCHIPS: Mini fruit chews (Starburst Minis) and green fruit chews (Jolly Rancher Green Apple)

USB POWER: green fruit chews (Jolly Rancher Green Apple)

SATA PLUGS: blue fruit chews (Jolly Rancher Blue Raspberry)

GRAPHICS CARD SLOTS: Chocolate caramel cookie bar (Twix)

BATTERY: Mini chocolate peppermint patty (York Peppermint Patties Minis)

CAPACITORS: Small chewy candies (Jujubes)

PLUGS: Mini chocolate wafer bars (Kit Kat Minis)

NORTH BRIDGE AND SOUTH BRIDGE: Chocolate peanut butter bar (Reese's)

RIBBON TO CONNECT N/S BRIDGES: Sour candy belts (Airheads Xtremes)

PROCESSOR: Chocolate square (Ghirardelli) and milk chocolate bar (Hershey's)

RAM SLOTS: Chocolate wafer bar (Kit Kat)

2. Scoop the remaining tub of white frosting into 3 decorating bags fitted with #2, #3, and #5 tips, and pipe on the electrical pathway details Ⓔ.

3. Using the reserved green frosting (in the decorating bag fitted with a #4B tip), pipe green trim at the bottom of the cake Ⓕ.

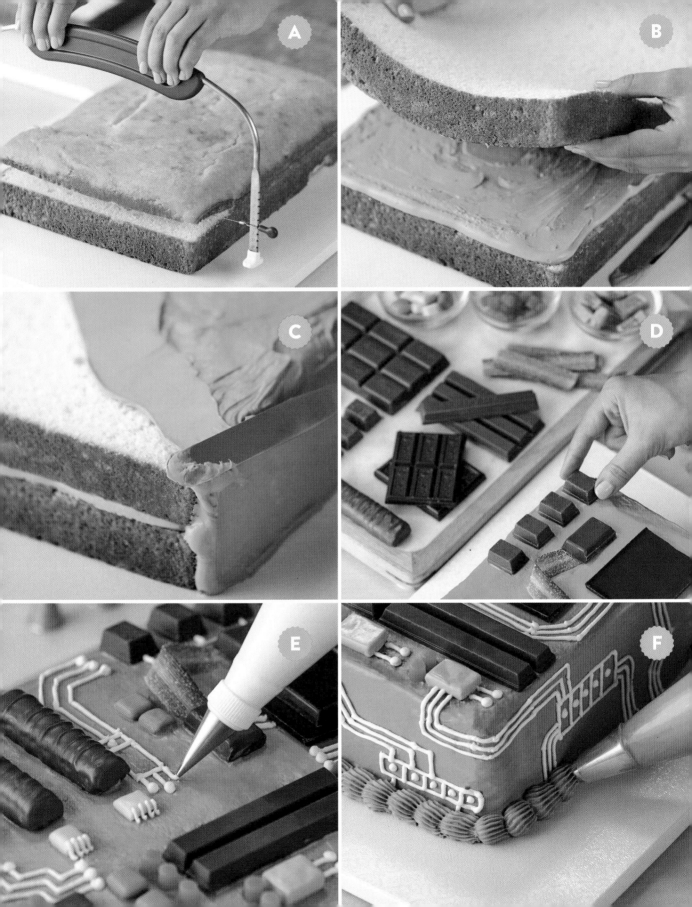

COLOR CODE
COOKIES

CODE TELLS COMPUTERS HOW TO DISPLAY websites the way you want. I built my first website using HTML code in middle school, altering the colors of each page with lines of binary: a system of computer language that uses only 1s and 0s. I've written the binary code that represents its icing color on each cookie. Anyone can learn to code—just grab a cookie and try it!

THE THINGS YOU'LL NEED

Vanilla Almond Sugar Cookie dough (page 34)

2 batches Royal Icing (page 36)

Food coloring gels: red, orange, electric yellow, leaf green, sky blue, purple, and black

Baking sheet

2¾-inch square cookie cutter

9 decorating bags

Nine #2 decorating tips

RO TIP

EVERY COLOR HAS A BINARY CODE. *Use any color you'd like (search for the code you need online).*

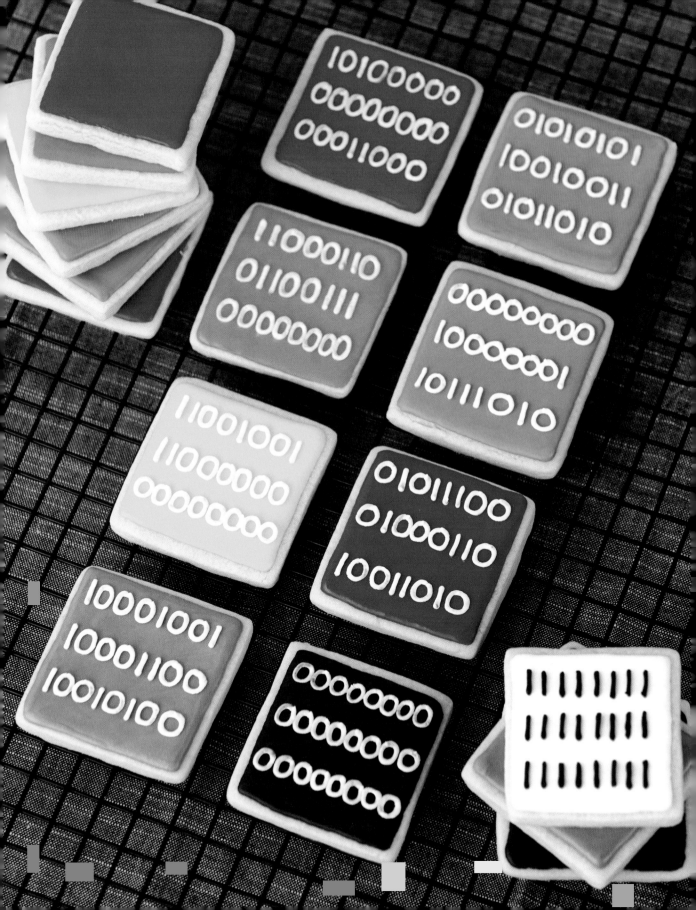

1. Preheat the oven to 350°F. Line a baking sheet with parchment paper.

2. Prepare the Vanilla Almond Sugar Cookie dough.

3. On a lightly floured surface, roll out the dough ¼ inch thick and cut out as many cookies as you can using the square cookie cutter Ⓐ.

4. Place the cookies 1 inch apart on the lined baking sheet Ⓑ.

5. Bake until the cookies are firm to the touch but not browned at the edges, 7 to 9 minutes.

6. Let the cookies cool on the baking sheet for 2 minutes, then transfer to a wire rack to cool completely.

~~~~~~~~~~ **TIME TO DECORATE!** ~~~~~~~~~~

1. While the cookies are cooling, make the Royal Icing and divide it among 9 bowls. Tint each bowl with a different food coloring Ⓒ: red, orange, electric yellow, leaf green, sky blue, purple, black, and gray (just add a small amount of black to white icing). Leave one bowl plain white.

2. Scoop the icings into separate decorating bags fitted with #2 tips.

3. Outline your cookies with the various colored icings Ⓓ.

4. Once the outlines have hardened, fill in the centers with more icing Ⓔ. You can use a toothpick to help spread it evenly.

5. Pipe on the binary RGB code for each color cookie using the white or black icing Ⓕ.

   I converted the decimal codes for my RGB colors to their binary codes:

   RED: 10100000,00000000,00011000

   ORANGE: 11000110,01100111,00000000

   YELLOW: 11001001,11000000,00000000

   GRAY: 10001001,10001100,10010100

   GREEN: 01010101,10010011,01011010

   BLUE: 00000000,10000001,10111010

   PURPLE: 01011100,01000110,10011010

   BLACK: 00000000,00000000,00000000

   WHITE: 11111111,11111111,11111111

FLASH DRIVE
CRISPY TREATS

I LIKE TO MAKE DESSERTS OUT of homemade Rice Krispies Treats because they're so easy to mold. You can sculpt them into nearly any shape, or create designs using cookie cutters! These snacks look like flash drives, which store data using flash memory. I use flash drives on a daily basis, transporting pictures and videos wherever I go—that's why I made an ode to them with these sweet treats.

THE THINGS YOU'LL NEED

3 tablespoons salted butter, plus more for greasing the pan

10 ounces marshmallows

6 cups puffed rice cereal (Rice Krispies)

4 bags (12 ounces each) Candy Melts (Wilton): red, white, black, and yellow

Royal Icing (page 36)

Black food coloring gel

9 x 13-inch metal baking pan

2 x 3-inch rectangle cookie cutter (2 inches deep)

1½-inch square cookie cutter (1 inch deep)

Lollipop sticks

2 foam blocks

2 decorating bags

#2 decorating tip

#3 decorating tip

Lightning bolt template (page 253 or QR code on page 196)

RO TIP

CANDY MELTS WILL HARDEN AT *room temperature, but to speed up the process, put them in the fridge or freezer.*

1. Grease a 9 x 13-inch metal baking pan.

2. In a saucepan, melt the 3 tablespoons butter over medium heat. Add the marshmallows and stir until they are completely melted.

3. Add the Rice Krispies and mix together until well coated.

4. Scoop the mixture into the prepared baking pan. Use a sheet of wax paper to press the top flat and even. Let the cereal treats cool to room temperature.

5. Remove the cereal treats from the pan. Using the cookie cutters, cut out rectangles and squares—the same number for each shape Ⓐ.

6. Insert a lollipop stick into each rectangle and square. Place in the freezer for 20 minutes to harden.

~~~~ TIME TO DECORATE! ~~~~

1. In the microwave or a double boiler, melt the red Candy Melts. Dip in the rectangles, making sure to cover them completely. Stand the dipped rectangles upright in a foam block to dry Ⓑ.

2. Melt the white and black Candy Melts together to make a gray color. (I use a ratio of 9 white melts to 1 black melt.) Dip in the square treats, making sure to cover them completely. Stand the dipped squares upright in a foam block to dry Ⓒ.

3. Once the coating is set, remove the lollipop sticks from the treats.

4. Use a small amount of gray melts to attach the gray squares to the red rectangles Ⓓ.

5. Make the Royal Icing and tint it with black food coloring until it is solid black. Scoop the icing into a decorating bag fitted with a #2 tip and pipe small black squares onto the gray squares Ⓔ.

6. Use the QR code or trace the lightning bolt template (page 253) onto a piece of paper. Lay a piece of wax paper over the template.

7. Melt the yellow Candy Melts. Scoop the melted candy into a decorating bag fitted with a #3 tip. Trace and fill in the lightning bolt shapes. Place the lightning bolts in the freezer for 15 minutes to harden.

8. Once the lightning bolts are set, use a dab of yellow candy to carefully stick them onto your flash drives Ⓕ.

SCAN
for Lightning
Bolt Template

HASHTAG
COOKIES

HASHTAGS ARE USED TO SORT AND ORGANIZE words for search algorithms, but they are also a #socialmedialanguage all their own. Tag something with certain #keywords and lots of people might see it. Go ahead and make your own favorite #hashtags with your #BFF!

THE THINGS YOU'LL NEED

Vanilla Almond Sugar Cookie dough
  (page 34)

Royal Icing (page 36)

Purple food coloring gel

Purple sanding sugar

Baking sheet

Alphabet cookie cutters

Hashtag cookie cutter (template on
  page 253 or QR code on page 200)

Decorating bag

#2 decorating tip

RO·TIP·

YOU CAN USE A TOOTHPICK TO *help neaten up the edges of the cookies before baking.*

LET'S GET STARTED!

1. Preheat the oven to 350°F. Line a baking sheet with parchment paper.

2. Prepare the Vanilla Almond Sugar Cookie dough.

3. On a lightly floured surface, roll out the dough ¼ inch thick **A**.

4. Cut out letters and hashtags with the cookie cutters **B**. (If you don't have a hashtag cookie cutter, use the template on page 253 or the QR code to make a stencil.)

5. Place the cookies on the lined baking sheet **C** and bake until firm to the touch but not browned at the edges, 7 to 9 minutes.

6. Let the cookies cool on the baking sheet for 2 minutes, then transfer to a wire rack to cool completely.

SCAN
for Hashtag
Cookie
Template

TIME TO DECORATE!

1. Make the Royal Icing. Tint the icing with purple food coloring until you reach the desired shade of purple. Scoop the icing into a decorating bag fitted with a #2 tip, and outline the cookies **D**.

2. Once the outline hardens, fill the center with more purple icing **E**. You can use a toothpick to help spread it evenly.

3. While the icing is still wet, sprinkle the sanding sugar onto the cookies **F**.

4. Arrange your cookies into #FunHashtags!

POWER ON
POPS

THESE CAKE POPS ARE EMBLAZONED with the universal symbol for power, which tells operators a machine can be switched on and off. Go ahead and take a bite—you'll feel booted up in no time!

THE THINGS YOU'LL NEED

White Cake batter (page 25)

6 ounces cream cheese, at room temperature, or 1 tub (16 ounces) buttercream frosting

2 bags (12 ounces each) white Candy Melts (Wilton)

Royal Icing (page 36)

Leaf green food coloring gel

Green sanding sugar

9 x 13-inch metal baking pan

Baking sheet

Lollipop sticks

Foam block

Decorating bag

#3 decorating tip

PRO TIP FOR SMOOTH-LOOKING CAKE POPS, YOU CAN *add a little vegetable oil or some oil flakes to thin out the Candy Melts.*

1. Bake the White Cake batter in a 9 x 13-inch metal baking pan as directed. Let the cake cool in the pan.

2. In a bowl, crumble the cake with your fingers.

3. Add the cream cheese or frosting to the crumbled cake and mix until evenly combined. (Use cream cheese if you like your cake balls more tart or use the frosting if you like them sweeter.)

4. Line a baking sheet with wax paper. Roll the cake mixture into balls (about 1½ inches) and place them on the lined baking sheet.

5. Freeze the cake balls until set, about 30 minutes.

6. In the microwave or a double boiler, melt a small amount (about 5 ounces) of the Candy Melts.

7. Dip the ends of the lollipop sticks in the melted candy (it acts as an adhesive) and push the sticks halfway into the cake balls A.

8. Place the cake pops in the refrigerator for about 30 minutes to chill.

TIME TO DECORATE!

1. Melt the remaining white Candy Melts.

2. Dip the cake pops into the melts, making sure to cover them completely. Let the excess candy drip back into the bowl B.

3. Stand the cake pops up in a foam block to dry C.

4. Make the Royal Icing, and tint it with leaf green food coloring until you reach the desired shade of green. Scoop the icing into a decorating bag fitted with a #3 tip.

5. Pipe one vertical line at the front of each cake pop D.

6. Pipe a semicircle with the ends near, but not touching, the vertical line to complete the "Power On" button icon E.

7. While the icing is still wet, lightly sprinkle the pop with the green sanding sugar F.

EMOTICON
COOKIES

EMOTICONS ARE TINY CHARACTERS WITH LOTS of personality. While made popular on cell phones and in social media, they didn't get their start on keyboards: Morse code operators would send numbers to one another that meant "love and kisses." I personally prefer the smiley face emoticon—he's always having a good time, even when you take a bite out of him.

～ THE THINGS YOU'LL NEED ～

Vanilla Almond Sugar Cookie dough
(page 34)

2 batches Royal Icing (page 36)

Food coloring gels: mint green, lemon yellow, electric orange, sky blue, electric pink, and black

Baking sheet

2½-inch round cookie cutter

6 decorating bags

Five #5 decorating tips

#3 decorating tip

RO TIP

WHEN USING MULTIPLE ICINGS *on the same cookie, give each icing time to set so they don't run together.*

1. Preheat the oven to 350°F. Line a baking sheet with parchment paper.

2. Prepare the Vanilla Almond Sugar Cookie dough.

3. On a lightly floured surface, roll out the dough ¼ inch thick.

4. Cut out as many cookies as you can using the round cookie cutter (A).

5. Place the cookies 1 inch apart on the lined baking sheet (B) and bake until firm to the touch but not browned at the edges, 7 to 9 minutes.

6. Let the cookies cool on the baking sheet for 2 minutes, then transfer to a wire rack to cool completely.

TIME TO DECORATE!

1. Make the Royal Icing. Divide the icing among 6 bowls. Tint 5 bowls with different food colorings: mint green, lemon yellow, electric orange, sky blue, and electric pink (C). (Reserve the last bowl for step 4.)

2. Scoop the colored icings into separate decorating bags fitted with #5 tips, and outline the cookies (D).

3. Once the outline hardens, fill in the center with more icing (E). You can use a toothpick to help spread it evenly.

4. Tint the reserved bowl of icing with black food coloring until it is solid black. Scoop the icing into a decorating bag fitted with a #3 tip and pipe on your emoticon faces (F).

CHEESEBURGER
CUPCAKES

A GOOD JOKE CAN SPREAD THROUGHOUT the internet between the time you go to bed and the time you wake up, leading to an inbox filled with funny pictures. These viral images are often referred to as "memes" and have been a mainstay of the internet for many years. Some of the earliest memes were jokes about cheeseburgers and have been transformed into these tasty cupcakes. You can haz as many as you'd like.

THE THINGS YOU'LL NEED

Brownie batter (page 30)

Butter Cake batter (page 23)

1 tub (16 ounces) buttercream frosting

Food coloring gels: yellow and red

Sweetened flaked coconut

Green liquid food coloring

White sprinkles

9 x 13-inch metal baking pan

Muffin tin(s)

Cupcake liners

2⅓-inch round cookie cutter

2 decorating bags

#48 decorating tip

#10 decorating tip

Baking tweezers (optional)

RO·TIP·

YOU CAN EVEN CUT STRIPS OF *pound cake to look like fries!*

1. Bake the Brownie batter in a 9 x 13-inch metal baking pan as directed. Let cool completely in the pan.

2. Preheat the oven to 350°F. Line 24 cups of 2 muffin tins with paper liners. (Or use 1 muffin tin and bake in two batches.)

3. Prepare the Butter Cake batter and divide it among the muffin cups, filling each one two-thirds full.

4. Bake until a wooden pick inserted in the center of a cupcake comes out clean, 18 to 20 minutes.

5. Let the cupcakes cool completely before decorating.

6. Use the round cookie cutter to cut out "hamburger patties" from the brownies Ⓐ.

7. Halve the cupcakes horizontally with a straight edge (not serrated) knife Ⓑ.

8. Place the brownie burgers on the bottom halves of the cupcakes Ⓒ.

TIME TO DECORATE!

1. Mix half of the buttercream frosting with yellow food coloring until it is the color of cheese. Scoop the frosting into a decorating bag fitted with a #48 tip and pipe it to look like cheese slices on your patties.

2. Tint the other half of the buttercream frosting with red food coloring until you reach the desired shade of bright red. Scoop the frosting into a decorating bag fitted with a #10 tip and pipe it to look like a tomato on top of the cheese Ⓓ.

3. Mix the flaked coconut with liquid green food coloring until it is light green, resembling lettuce Ⓔ. Sprinkle the coconut flakes on top of the red frosting.

4. Place the top half of each cupcake on top.

5. Scatter white sprinkles on top of the cupcakes to look like sesame seeds. I use baking tweezers for more control Ⓕ.

AWKWARD PENGUIN
COOKIES

THE AWKWARD PENGUIN IS ONE of my favorite memes because I relate to a lot of the socially awkward situations he finds himself in. I used to feel really awkward in high school, but overcame it by learning to laugh. Awkward penguin is a hallmark of those times, yet he forever waddles on, mustering the courage to talk to his crush or order a pizza. I think he could use some friends! Luckily this recipe produces several penguins, so you can make a whole bunch of friends to keep him company no matter how awkward the situation gets. Then you can eat all of them. Awkward.

THE THINGS YOU'LL NEED

Vanilla Almond Sugar Cookie dough
   (page 34)

Food coloring gels: black and orange

Egg wash: 1 egg beaten with 2
   tablespoons water

Royal Icing (page 36)

Baking sheet

3 decorating bags

#2 decorating tip

Two #1 decorating tips

RO·TIP· IF YOUR COOKIES CHANGE SHAPE WHILE *you are cutting the log, you can use your fingers to reshape them on the baking sheet.*

1. Prepare the Vanilla Almond Sugar Cookie dough.

2. Divide the dough in half, and tint one half with black food coloring until it is solid black. Tightly wrap the black dough in plastic wrap and place it in the refrigerator.

3. Roll the untinted dough into a log 1½ inches in diameter and 18 inches long Ⓐ. Tightly wrap the dough in plastic wrap and place it in the freezer for 8 hours.

4. Remove the plastic wrap from the frozen dough log. Brush the log with the egg wash (it acts as an adhesive).

5. Roll out the black dough to a rectangle ¼ inch thick and about 7 x 18 inches. Place the dough log along one long edge of the black dough and roll them together. The black dough should overlap for about 25 percent of the rolled-up log, making that part of the dough log thicker than the rest. The thicker portion will be the penguin heads Ⓑ.

6. Tightly wrap the dough log in plastic wrap and place it in the freezer for 30 minutes.

7. Preheat the oven to 350°F. Line a baking sheet with parchment paper.

8. Cut the dough log into ¼-inch-thick cookie slices Ⓒ.

9. Arrange the cookies on the lined baking sheet and bake until firm to the touch, 7 to 9 minutes.

10. Let the cookies cool on the baking sheet for 2 minutes, then transfer to a wire rack to cool completely.

TIME TO DECORATE!

1. Make the Royal Icing and divide it among 3 bowls. Tint one bowl orange, one black, and leave one bowl white. Scoop the white icing into a decorating bag fitted with a #2 tip and the colored icings into bags fitted with #1 tips.

2. Pipe on the penguin eyes with the white icing Ⓓ.

3. Pipe on the beak and the feet with the orange icing Ⓔ.

4. Pipe on the eye and wing details with the black icing Ⓕ.

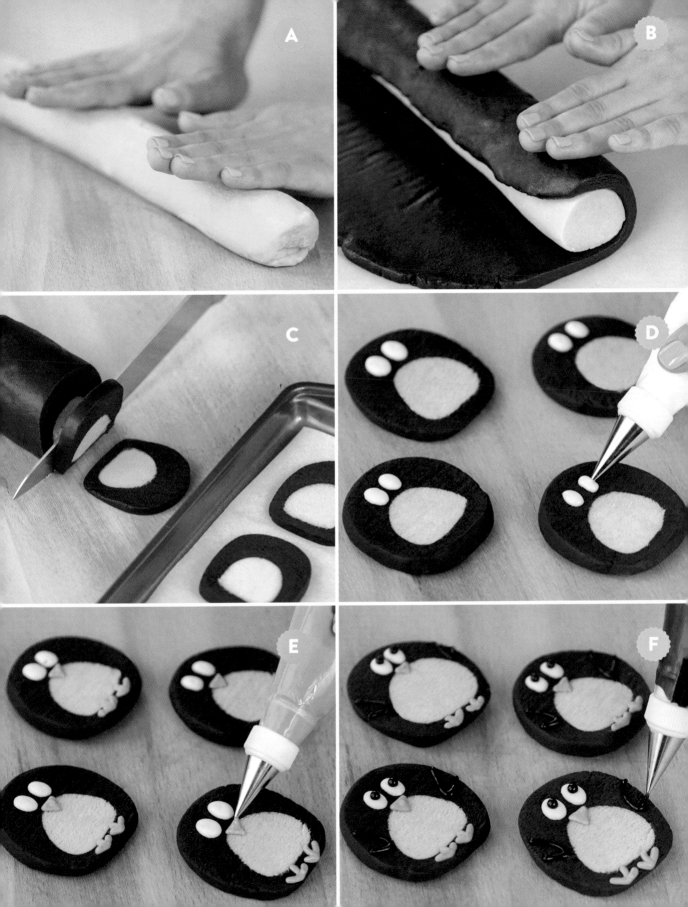

WI-FI
CHEESECAKE

WI-FI HELPS PEOPLE ALL OVER STAY CONNECTED to the internet from almost anywhere. I designed this cheesecake to look like a Wi-Fi symbol when you cut into it. Once you've made this recipe, connecting to the internet will be a piece of cake!

THE THINGS YOU'LL NEED

New York–Style Cheesecake filling and crust (page 28)

Electric blue food coloring gel

9-inch springform pan

Decorating bag

#12 decorating tip

IF YOUR CHEESECAKE IS CRACKING, TRY BAKING IT *in a water bath to add moisture and more gentle heat while baking. For a water bath, wrap your cheesecake pan bottom and sides with aluminum foil, then place in a larger pan with about 1 inch of water to bake.*

1. Preheat the oven to 350°F.

2. Make the crust as directed, pressing the crumb mixture 2 inches up the sides of the 9-inch springform pan Ⓐ. Bake for 10 minutes to set the crust. Remove the pan from the oven to cool, but leave the oven on.

3. Make the filling as directed. Measure out and set aside 2 cups of the filling and pour the rest into the prepared crust and spread evenly Ⓑ.

4. Tint the reserved 2 cups of cheesecake mixture with electric blue food coloring until you reach the desired shade of blue Ⓒ.

5. Scoop the blue mixture into a decorating bag fitted with a #12 tip.

6. Pipe a 2-inch-diameter circle in the center of the cheesecake Ⓓ.

7. Pipe three concentric rings around the center circle Ⓔ.

8. Bake, cool, and chill as directed.

9. Cut the cheesecake into portions to resemble Wi-Fi signals Ⓕ.

CHAPTER SIX

GEEKY TREATS

· · ·

SMART
COOKIES

·

SMART COOKIE IS THE MASCOT of Nerdy Nummies. She works hard, studies hard, and might be a little bit of a teacher's pet. I designed her glasses to look like the first pair of reading glasses I ever owned. She's one smart cookie!

THE THINGS YOU'LL NEED

Royal Icing (page 36)

Food coloring gels: black and electric pink

Chocolate Chip Cookie dough (page 32), made without adding the chips (see step 5)

Smart Cookie eyeglasses template (page 253 or QR code on page 226)

3 decorating bags

#2 decorating tip

Two #1 decorating tips

Baking sheet

RO TIP

LET THE ICING EYEGLASSES HARDEN *at room temperature. Do not put them in the fridge or freezer.*

LET'S GET STARTED!

SCAN
for Smart Cookie
Eyeglasses
Template

1. Use the QR code or trace the Smart Cookie eyeglasses design onto a piece of paper to make a template (page 253). Lay a piece of wax paper over the template **A**.

2. Make one batch of Royal Icing, and tint it with black food coloring until it is solid black. Scoop the icing into a decorating bag fitted with a #2 tip and trace the eyeglasses onto the wax paper **B**.

3. Let the eyeglasses sit out at room temperature to harden, a minimum of 8 hours. (I like to make my eyeglasses the night before so they can sit overnight.)

4. Preheat the oven to 375°F.

5. Prepare the Chocolate Chip Cookie dough, but do not add the chocolate chips. Set the chips aside to be used later for decoration.

6. Take rounded tablespoons of the dough and roll them into balls. Place the balls 2 inches apart on an ungreased baking sheet.

7. Bake until golden brown, 7 to 9 minutes.

8. Let the cookies cool on the baking sheet for 1 minute, then transfer to a wire rack.

9. While the cookies are still warm, place 4 chocolate chips at the top and 2 near the bottom of each cookie leaving enough space for the eyeglasses **C**.

TIME TO DECORATE!

1. Make a second batch of Royal Icing and divide it between 2 bowls. Tint one bowl with black food coloring until it is solid black, and tint the other bowl with electric pink until it is a light pink. Scoop the icings into decorating bags fitted with #1 tips.

2. Carefully separate the eyeglasses from the wax paper and dab a little black icing onto the back of the eyeglasses before placing them on the cookies **D**.

3. Pipe on the eyes and smile using the black icing **E**.

4. Pipe on the cheeks using the pink icing **F**.

8-BIT HEART
COCOA

·

SIDE-OF-THE-CUP COOKIES ARE A REALLY FUN idea for a morning or evening snack. You can cut a notch into your favorite cookie, like these 8-bit pixel hearts, and pair it with any drink you want. Pixels are tiny squares of light that are used to make all kinds of designs and characters. Most early video games were animated using them, so we owe a lot to the little guys for making gaming special! Each pixel has a lot of—wait for it—heart!

THE THINGS YOU'LL NEED

Vanilla Almond Sugar Cookie dough
(page 34)

Royal Icing (page 36)

Red food coloring gel

Hot cocoa

Whipped cream and ground cinnamon
(optional)

Baking sheet

8-bit heart cookie cutter (template on
page 253 or QR code on page 230)

Decorating bag

#1 decorating tip

RO TIP

CUT YOUR NOTCHES BIG ENOUGH *to leave room for the cookie dough to expand while baking and still fit on the side of your mug.*

LET'S GET STARTED!

1. Preheat the oven to 350°F. Line a baking sheet with parchment paper.

2. Prepare the Vanilla Almond Sugar Cookie dough.

3. On a lightly floured surface, roll out the dough ¼ inch thick **A**.

4. Cut out as many hearts as you can using the 8-bit heart cookie cutter **B**. (If you don't have an 8-bit heart cookie cutter, use the template on page 253 or the QR code to make a stencil.)

5. Place the cookies on the lined baking sheet and cut a notch in each cookie using a straight edge (not serrated) knife **C**. This will be the notch you use to place the cookie on the rim of your mug.

6. Bake the cookies until firm to the touch but not browned at the edges, 7 to 9 minutes.

7. Let the cookies cool on the baking sheet for 2 minutes, then transfer to a wire rack to cool completely.

SCAN
for 8-bit
Heart Cookie
Template

TIME TO DECORATE!

1. Make the Royal Icing. Tint the icing with red food coloring until it is a solid red. Scoop the icing into a decorating bag fitted with a #1 tip. Outline the cookies with the red icing **D**.

2. Once the outline hardens, fill in the center with more red icing **E**. You can use a toothpick to help spread it evenly.

3. Fill mugs with hot cocoa and place an 8-bit heart on the side of each mug **F**.

4. Optional: Top off the cocoa with some whipped cream and a sprinkle of cinnamon.

COMIC BOOK
COOKIES

•

I LOVE SEEING SOME OF MY favorite childhood comic books being adapted into movies and TV shows. They remind us that there's a hero inside everyone, even if we don't have super strength and can't fly faster than a speeding bullet. These cookies look like comic book onomatopoeias—words that mimic sounds like BOOM and POW! They're classic action blurbs with a tasty twist! Try making your favorites—SNIKT!

THE THINGS YOU'LL NEED

Royal Icing (page 36)

Food coloring gels: red, yellow, and blue

Vanilla Almond Sugar Cookie dough (page 34)

Food color sprays: red, yellow, and blue

Explosion and cloud templates (page 253 or QR code on page 234)

4 decorating bags

Four #2 decorating tips

Four #1 decorating tips

Baking sheet

3½-inch round cookie cutter

3-inch square cookie cutter

Polka-dot stencil

RO·TIP

MAKE SURE THE COOKIE ICING *has completely hardened before decorating.*

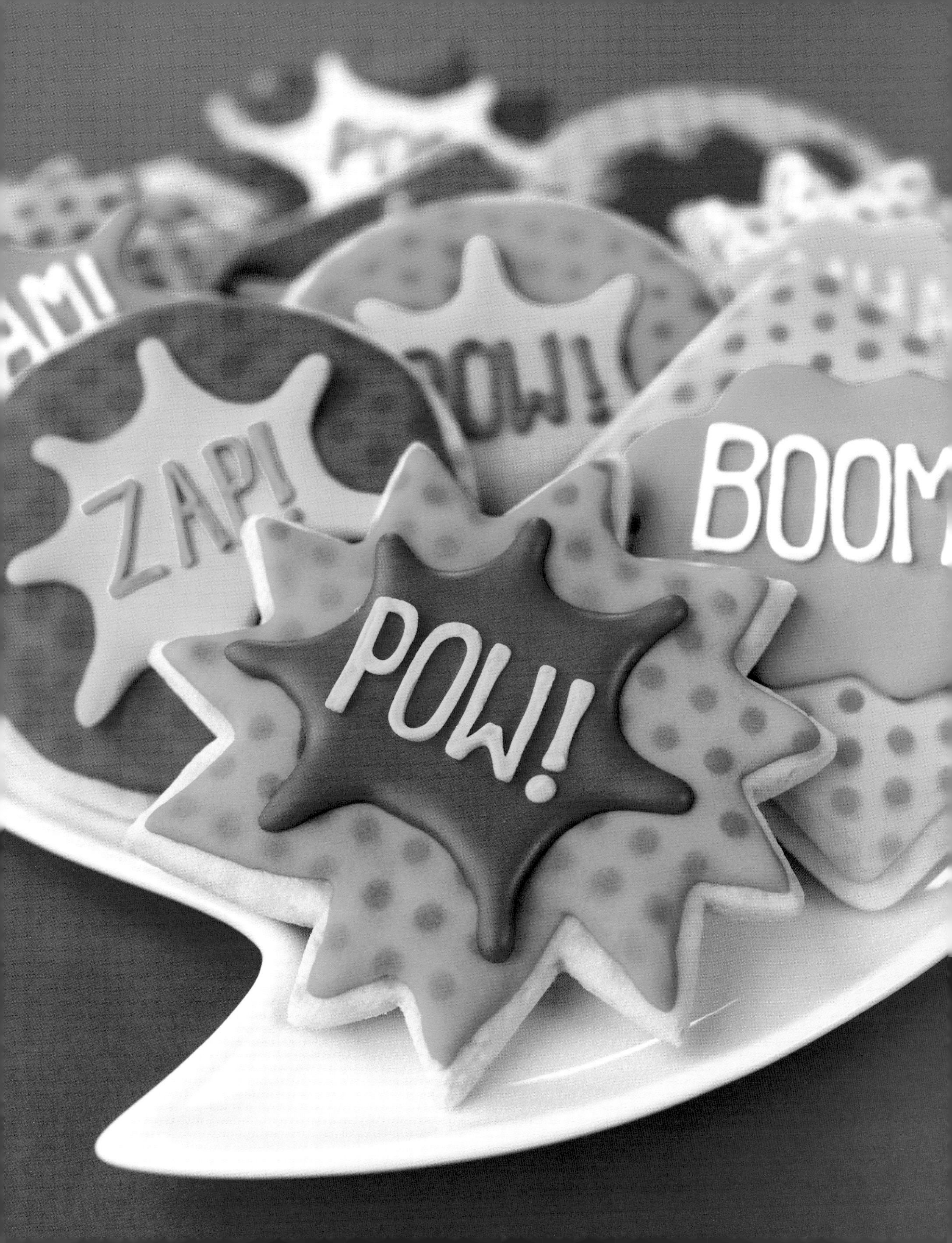

POW!
ZAP!
BOOM

LET'S GET STARTED!

1. Trace the explosion and cloud templates (page 253) onto a piece of paper or print using the QR code. Lay a piece of wax paper over the template.

2. Make the Royal Icing. Divide the icing among 4 bowls. Leave one bowl white and tint the others red, yellow, and blue. Scoop the icings into separate decorating bags fitted with #2 tips.

3. Pipe the explosion and cloud shapes onto the wax paper (A). Save the colored icing bags; you will use these again for more decorations.

4. Let the explosion and cloud shapes sit out at room temperature to harden, a minimum of 8 hours. (I like to do this the night before so they can sit overnight.)

5. Preheat the oven to 350°F. Line a baking sheet with parchment paper.

6. Prepare the Vanilla Almond Sugar Cookie dough.

7. On a lightly floured surface, roll out the dough ¼ inch thick. Using cookie cutters, cut out as many round, square, and explosion-shaped cookies as you can. For the explosion shape, use the corner of the square cookie cutter to cut points into a round cookie.

8. Place the cookies on the lined baking sheet and bake until firm to the touch but not browned at the edges, 7 to 9 minutes.

9. Let the cookies cool on the baking sheet for 2 minutes, then transfer to a wire rack to cool completely.

SCAN
for Explosion
and Cloud
Templates

TIME TO DECORATE!

1. Outline the cookies with the colored icings (B).

2. Fill in the outlines with colored icings (C). You can use a toothpick to help spread it evenly. Let the cookies sit at room temperature until the icing is completely hardened, about 1 hour.

3. Lay the polka-dot stencil over a cookie. Holding the food color spray can about 6 inches from the stencil, spray the food coloring on the dots. Mix and match the colors (D).

4. Carefully separate the explosion and cloud icing shapes from the wax paper. Stick them to the cookies with a dab of icing to act as an adhesive (E).

5. Switch the tips on the decorating bags to the #1 tips. Pipe on comic book action words like BOOM! POW! ZAP! KAPOW! POP! (F).

NERD BIRD
CUPCAKES

OWLS ARE A SYMBOL OF WISDOM and nobility; some even consider them benevolent protectors. In fantasy, they serve similar roles by transporting messages, giving hints, and keeping a watchful eye. Owls have real historic meaning and some serious geek cred, so it seems only natural to frost a few onto cupcakes and eat them. They've earned the official title of "Nerd Bird" in my book!

THE THINGS YOU'LL NEED

White Cake batter (page 25)

1 tub (16 ounces) buttercream frosting

48 mini chocolate sandwich cookies (Mini Oreos)

Chocolate peanut butter candy (Reese's Pieces): 48 brown and 24 orange

Sliced almonds

1 tub (16 ounces) chocolate frosting

Muffin tin(s)

Brown cupcake liners

Baking tweezers (optional)

Decorating bag

#1 decorating tip

RO TIP

DON'T TRUST THESE BIRDS *to deliver your messages— they rarely make it out of the kitchen.*

1. Bake the White Cake, following the directions for cupcakes and lining the muffin cups with brown paper liners.

2. Let the cupcakes cool completely before decorating.

TIME TO DECORATE!

1. Frost the cupcakes with buttercream frosting **A**.

2. Twist apart the Mini Oreos. On the cream side, place a brown Reese's Piece **B**.

3. Place the candy-topped Oreos on the cupcakes for eyes **C**.

4. Set an orange Reese's Piece upright in between the eyes for a beak **D**. You can use baking tweezers for more control.

5. Add the sliced almonds around the edges of the cupcakes to look like feathers **E**.

6. Scoop the chocolate frosting into a decorating bag fitted with a #1 tip, and pipe on chest feather details **F**.

GLASSES
COOKIES

·

THIS IS A CLASSIC HOLIDAY DESSERT called stained-glass sugar cookies—now with a geeky twist. I've always loved glasses and get really excited when I try on a new pair. Glasses work by bending light to improve the person's vision, so if you wear them, you're really walking around with science on your face! These glasses are for eating, but don't let that stop you from wearing them. Just remember that if anyone calls you "four eyes," it means you've got twice as many!

THE THINGS YOU'LL NEED

Vanilla Almond Sugar Cookie dough (page 34)

Black food coloring gel

Clear hard candies

6 ounces chocolate chips

Baking sheet

Eyeglasses cookie cutter (template on page 253 or QR code on page 242)

1⅛-inch round cookie cutter

⅞-inch round cookie cutter

Eyeglasses temple template (page 253 or QR code on page 242)

Rimmed baking sheet

Heatproof glass measuring cup (Pyrex)

RO TIP YOU CAN USE ANY COLOR HARD CANDIES *to customize the lens color of your glasses.*

LET'S GET STARTED!

1. Preheat the oven to 350°F. Line a baking sheet with parchment paper.

2. Prepare the Vanilla Almond Sugar Cookie dough. Mix in black food coloring to tint the dough solid black.

3. On a lightly floured surface, roll out the dough ¼ inch thick.

4. Cut out as many cookies as you can using the eyeglasses cookie cutter Ⓐ. (If you don't have an eyeglasses cookie cutter, use the template on page 253 or the QR code to make a stencil.)

5. Using the 1⅛-inch round cookie cutter, cut out the centers of the glasses. Use the ⅞-inch round cookie cutter to help shape the detail of the lens area Ⓑ. Gather the scraps of dough and save for cutting out the eyeglasses temples.

6. On a lightly floured surface, roll out the dough scraps ¼ inch thick. Use the eyeglasses temple template (page 253) or the QR code to make a stencil. Place the stencil on the dough and use a small sharp knife to cut around the template Ⓒ.

7. Place the cookies on the lined baking sheet Ⓓ and bake until firm to the touch, 7 to 9 minutes.

8. Let the cookies cool on the baking sheet for 2 minutes, then transfer to a wire rack to cool completely.

SCAN for Eyeglasses Template

SCAN for Eyeglasses Temple Template

TIME TO DECORATE!

1. Line a rimmed baking sheet with wax paper. Place the cookies on the lined baking sheet.

2. Microwave the clear hard candies in a heatproof glass measuring cup for 45 seconds, then stir immediately to get rid of any bubbles. Quickly and carefully pour the hard candy liquid into the lens holes of the eyeglasses Ⓔ.

3. Let the candy harden for 5 minutes.

4. In the microwave or a double boiler, melt the chocolate and use it as an adhesive to attach the temples to the eyeglasses Ⓕ. Hold in place until the chocolate hardens.

TEXTBOOK
S'MORES

I WANNA READ S'MORE! HERE'S A SIMPLE TREAT that's perfect to pack in your lunchbox or for an afterschool snack. They can be designed to look like your favorite academic subjects—mine were science, drama, and math! It's fun to be a lifelong learner, so fill up on a s'more and dive into a good book!

THE THINGS YOU'LL NEED

Vegetable oil, for greasing the pans

3 cups granulated sugar

1¼ cups light corn syrup

Pinch of salt

4 envelopes (¼ ounce each) unflavored gelatin

1 tablespoon vanilla extract

2 cups powdered sugar, for dusting

30 graham crackers (Honey Maid)

12 ounces milk chocolate

6 ounces white chocolate

Two 9 x 13-inch metal baking pans

Candy thermometer

Sieve

2-inch square cookie cutter

2 decorating bags

#2 decorating tip

#1 decorating tip

RO TIP

YOU CAN USE YOUR FAVORITE KIND *of chocolate for these treats.*

1. Brush two 9 x 13-inch metal baking pans with the oil and line with parchment paper, leaving a 2-inch overhang on the narrower sides. Brush the parchment paper with the oil.

2. In a medium saucepan, combine the granulated sugar, corn syrup, salt, and ¾ cup water over high heat. Bring to a boil, stirring the mixture constantly.

3. Place a candy thermometer in the pan and continue cooking until the sugar mixture reaches 238°F.

4. Meanwhile, pour ¾ cup cold water into a bowl. Sprinkle the gelatin over the water and let soften for 5 minutes.

5. Once the sugar mixture reaches 238°F, pour it into the gelatin mixture and beat it with an electric mixer on low speed. Gradually increase the speed to high, beating until the mixture is very stiff, about 12 minutes. Beat in the vanilla.

6. Pour the mixture into the two lined pans and smooth the tops with a spatula. Let the marshmallows sit uncovered until completely firm, about 3 hours.

7. Sift a layer of powdered sugar on top of the marshmallows and a work surface.

8. Remove the marshmallows from the pans and flip over onto the prepared work surface, then remove the parchment paper. Sift a layer of powdered sugar on the top of the marshmallows so all sides are covered (A).

9. Use the square cookie cutter or a sharp knife to cut out 24 marshmallow squares (B). Dip the cookie cutter or knife into powdered sugar between each use to keep the marshmallows from sticking.

10. Break 24 graham cracker sheets in half into squares—these will be the front and back covers of your books. Break 6 graham cracker sheets into quarters—these will be the spines of your books (C).

TIME TO DECORATE!

1. In the microwave or a double boiler, melt the milk chocolate and scoop it into a decorating bag fitted with a #2 tip. Using the melted chocolate as an adhesive, attach the graham crackers to the marshmallows to create your books (D).

2. Pipe on cover and side details with the milk chocolate (E).

3. Melt the white chocolate and scoop it into a decorating bag fitted with a #1 tip. Pipe on the book titles with the white chocolate (F).

• ACKNOWLEDGMENTS •

First I would like to thank all my VIEWERS, LOYAL SUBSCRIBERS, and the FANSINO FAMILY! I wouldn't be where I am today without you. You inspire my creativity and remind me each and every day that anything is possible.

YOUTUBE and GOOGLE, for giving me the opportunity to share my creativity with the world and be a part of an amazing online community.

All of my FRIENDS—your immense patience and optimism through this entire process kept me going when even coffee wasn't enough.

WINNY and JEN, for flying in from Seattle every month with a fantastic attitude and Hot Spicy Cheetos in hand, to help with anything and everything.

My photographer, MICHAEL SCHMIDT. You are extremely talented and I can't thank you enough for putting in so many long days and shooting countless photos for this book. You've done it all, from prop design, food styling, filming *Nerdy Nummies*, to now making our first cookbook.

My favorite sister, MOLLY LU, for keeping me going. You are the Pepper Pots to my Ro-ny Stark.

GREG BAILEY, for kicking butt and taking names every day. Thank you for keeping us fueled up with delicious grilled dinners and your positive energy.

GEOFF BAILEY: What don't you do? You literally flew in from out of state to help put out fires. From recipe development, testing, proofreading, and store runs to all the late nights prep baking. You're the man!

MOM & DAD, for being my lifelong cheerleaders! Dad, you taught me a strong work ethic that I use every day. Mom, you taught me to find happiness in everything I do. Your joyfulness is infectious. Also, thank you for making my awesome 8-bit heart apron (left).

JARED ROSEN, Jare-Bear! Thank you for staying up late to collaborate with the team on multiple occasions. So many great memories were made while coming up with funny food puns. #BlastOffToOuterTaste

My YouTube video editor, MATT JONES, for making me look like I know what I'm doing on the show. You are a wizard. Love having you on the team!

MARISSA MATTEO, for your advice, guidance, and willingness to embark on this cookbook adventure with me.

My literary agent, ERIN MALONE, for your enthusiasm and dedication to this project. Thanks for teaching me all about the publishing process.

RYAN PASTOREK, for always having my back.

My publisher, JUDITH CURR, and editor, JOHANNA CASTILLO, for giving me the opportunity to write this cookbook. Thank you for believing in me and my vision from our very first conversation. You made all my ideas a reality.

My business partner, manager, and so much more, MIKE LAMOND. You believed in me unconditionally before I even made my first video. Your encouragement to follow my dreams and make a YouTube channel completely changed my life. None of this would have been possible without your guidance and support from the very beginning. I am excited to be on this journey with you and can't wait to see what the future holds. Thank you for everything.

And most important, my dog COOKIE for keeping me company, never sharing my baking secrets, and making me smile. And, no . . . you can't eat this book!

• CONVERSION CHART •

MEASUREMENTS & TEMPERATURES

Cup to Tablespoon to Teaspoon to Milliliters

1 cup = 16 tablespoons = 48 teaspoons = 240 ml

¾ cup = 12 tablespoons = 36 teaspoons = 180 ml

⅔ cup = 11 tablespoons = 32 teaspoons = 160 ml

½ cup = 8 tablespoons = 24 teaspoons = 120 ml

⅓ cup = 5 tablespoons = 16 teaspoons = 80 ml

¼ cup = 4 tablespoons = 12 teaspoons = 60 ml

1 tablespoon = 15 ml

1 teaspoon = 5 ml

Cup to Fluid Ounces

1 cup = 8 fluid ounces

¾ cup = 6 fluid ounces

⅔ cup = 5 fluid ounces

½ cup = 4 fluid ounces

⅓ cup = 3 fluid ounces

¼ cup = 2 fluid ounces

Fahrenheit to Celsius (°F To °C)

500°F = 260°C

475°F = 245°C

450°F = 235°C

425°F = 220°C

400°F = 205°C

375°F = 190°C

350°F = 180°C

325°F = 160°C

300°F = 150°C

275°F = 135°C

250°F = 120°C

225°F = 107°C

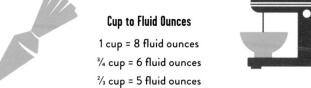

BASIC INGREDIENTS

All-Purpose Flour (Unsifted)

1 cup flour = 120 grams

¾ cup flour = 90 grams

½ cup flour = 60 grams

¼ cup flour = 30 grams

Granulated Sugar

1 cup sugar = 200 grams

¾ cup sugar = 150 grams

⅔ cup sugar = 135 grams

½ cup sugar = 100 grams

⅓ cup sugar = 70 grams

¼ cup sugar = 50 grams

Powdered Sugar (Unsifted)

1 cup powdered sugar = 120 grams

¾ cup powdered sugar = 120 grams

½ cup powdered sugar = 60 grams

¼ cup powdered sugar = 30 grams

Butter

1 cup butter = 2 sticks = 8 ounces = 227 grams

½ cup butter = 1 stick = 4 ounces = 113 grams

Heavy Cream

1 cup heavy cream = 235 grams

¾ cup heavy cream = 175 grams

½ cup heavy cream = 115 grams

¼ cup heavy cream = 60 grams

1 tablespoon heavy cream = 15 grams

• RESOURCE GUIDE •

BAKING SUPPLIES

Kitchen Krafts

P.O. Box 442
Waukon, IA 52172
(800) 776-0575
www.kitchenkrafts.com

Wide variety of decorating and baking supplies.

Sur La Table

(800) 243-0852
www.surlatable.com

Bakeware and tiered cake stands.

Wilton Industries

2240 West 75th Street
Woodbridge, IL 60517
(800) 794-5866
www.wilton.com

A wide variety of baking supplies, including Candy Melts, food coloring, paper liners, bakeware, assorted sprinkles, sugars, and much more. Products available in many craft, party, and grocery stores.

CRAFT & PARTY SUPPLY STORES

Michaels Stores

(800) 637-6050
www.michaels.com

A wide variety of craft supplies and cake-decorating supplies, including Wilton products.

Fred & Friends

www.fredandfriends.com

Variety of molds, baking, and funny party supplies.

CANDIES

Dylan's Candy Bar

(888) 359-2676
www.dylanscandybar.com

A wide variety of candies, including seasonal offerings.

Sweet Factory

2000 East Winston Road
Anaheim, CA 92806
(877) 817-9338
www.sweetfactory.com

A great selection of hard-to-find candies. Online and retail locations nationwide.

· TEMPLATES ·

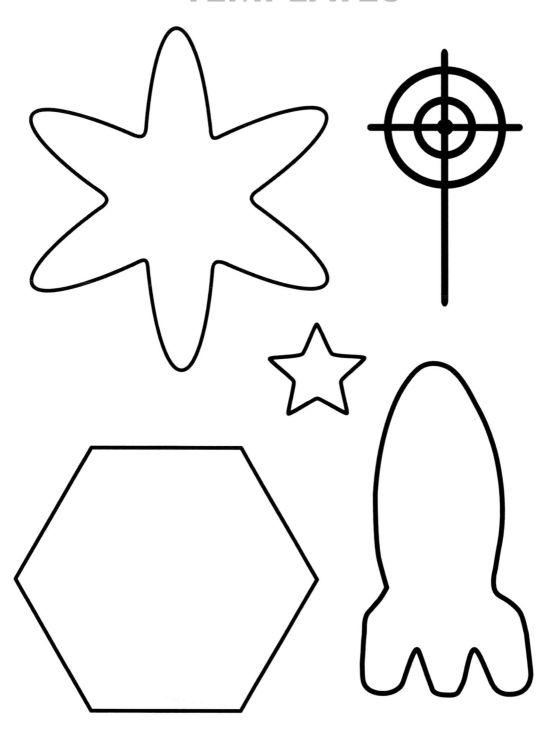

• INDEX •

• ABOUT THE AUTHOR •

ROSANNA PANSINO is the creator and host of *Nerdy Nummies*, the internet's most popular baking show. She is a Washington native who, upon graduating college, moved to Los Angeles to start her own production company. Pansino launched *Nerdy Nummies* in late 2011 and the show's audience grew very quickly. Her videos have been viewed more than 1 billion times—making Rosanna one of the most-watched personalities on YouTube. *The Nerdy Nummies Cookbook* is her first book.

SOCIAL MEDIA

youtube.com/rosannapansino

@rosannapansino

facebook.com/rosannapansino

@rosannapansino

VISIT WEBSITE

WWW.ROSANNAPANSINO.COM

FOR ALL THINGS NERDY NUMMIES